SOUTHERN SHAOLIN HUNG GAR KUNG FU CLASSICS SERIES

IRON THREAD

Priceless Heritage of Southern Shaolin
Inherited from the Past and Handed Down by Venerable Grandmaster

Lam Sai Wing

LAM SAI WING
IRON THREAD. SOUTHERN SHAOLIN HUNG GAR KUNG
FU CLASSICS SERIES

Chinese Martial Arts - Theory & Practice / Old & Rare Chinese
Books, Treatises, Manuscripts

shaolinkungfulibrary.com

/Old and Rare Chinese Books in English/

Shaolin Kung Fu Online Library

2024

IRON THREAD

SOUTHERN SHAOLIN HUNG GAR
KUNG FU CLASSICS SERIES

The translation is based on the edition by Juy Yu Jaai

(Hong Kong, 1957)

Lam Sai Wing
Andrew Timofeevich (Translator)

IRON THREAD. SOUTHERN SHAOLIN HUNG GAR KUNG FU CLASSICS SERIES

Compiled and edited by Andrew Timofeevich. Translated by Wang Ke Ze, Leonid Serbin and Oleg Korshunov.

Book design by Andrew Timofeevich and Olga Akimova.

Published by Shaolin Kung Fu Online Library

USA, 2024   IS

ISBN: 979-8-9919633-7-4

shaolinkungfulibrary.com

Disclaimer:

The author and publisher of this material are not responsible in any manner whatsoever for any injury whish may occur through reading or following the instruction in this manual. The activities, physical or otherwise, described in this material may be too strenuous or dangerous for some people, and the reader should consult a physician before engaging in them.

Venerable Grandmaster Lam Sai Wing

(1860 – 1943)

"Since my young years till now, for 50 years, I
have been learning from Masters. I am happy
that I have earned the love of my tutors who
passed on me the Shaolin Mastery..."

Jyu Yu Jaai

Editor and publisher of the first edition

(Hong Kong, 1957)

About the Author[1]

Lam Sai Wing (1861 - 1943) was born in the district of *Nan Hai, Guangdong* province. Followed the customs of ancestors and learnt the tradition of Martial Arts in his family, proceeded to learn from tutors *Lam Fook Sing, Wong Fei Hung,* and *Wu Gum Sin.*

Indulged in persistent training, achieved great mastership in the Martial Arts. Founded *Wu Ben Tang* ("The Hall of Fundamental Study") in *Guangzhou (Canton)* where he taught the Martial Arts. During his life brought up more than 10,000 followers.

Toward the end of the *Qing* dynasty (1644 - 1911) gained the first place at large competitions that took place at the *Dongjiao* ground. Thanks to it, with great pleasure, *Lam Sai Wing* received a silver medal handed to him by *Dr. Sun Yat-Sen*[2] himself as a token of the recognition of his great services and successes.

In the years followed, taking images and characters of the Tiger and the Crane as a base, as well as techniques of *Hung Gar Kuen*[3] and *Fo Kuen*[4] styles, he founded a new school *Fu Hok Seung Ying Kuen* ("The Double Form of the Tiger and the Crane").

---

[1] An article from *ZHONG GUO WU SHU ZEN MING CI DIAN* - Dictionary "Well-known Masters of the Chinese Wu Shu" edited by Chang Cang and Zhou Li Chang.

[2] *Sun Yat-Sen* (his other names: *Sun Zhongshan*, Sun Wen) (1866 - 1925), a Chinese revolutionary democrat, the leader of the Chinese Revolution of 1911 - 1913, the first (provisional) president of the Chinese Republic (1 January - 1 April, 1912). In 1912 founded *Guomindang* party.

[3] *Hung Gar Kuen* - "The fist of Hung family". This style was widespread in secret societies *Gelaohui* ("The union of the Elder Brother"), *Sandianhui* ("The Triad"), and others in the Southern China in the XIX - the beginning of the XX century. It is remarkable for its very high fighting efficiency. It takes its origin from the Southern Shaolin Tiger style.

[4] *Fo Kuen* - "The fist of Buddhist brotherhood" was practised in secret Buddhist sects in *Guangdong* province. That style also originates from the Southern Shaolin.

**Lam Sai Wing with his nephew Lam Cho (to the left of him) and
students (Hong Kong, 1932)**

Lived in his old years in *Hong Kong*[5] where he taught the Martial
Arts together with his favorite disciples *Juy Yu Jaai*, *Jeung Sai Biu*,
Lei Sai Fai, and others. Wrote books: *GUNG GEE FOOK FU
KUEN* ("Taming the Tiger"), *TID SIN KUEN* ("Iron Thread
Fist"), and *FU HOK SEUNG YING KUEN* ("The Double
Form of the Tiger and the Crane").

Marked a new epoch and a new school of Chinese Martial Arts,
in particular in the division of formal complexes *Tao Lu*. *Fu Hok
Seung Ying Kuen* is practiced on a large scale both in China and
abroad and the interest to it does not fall down. After the
formation of the People's Republic of China (1949) this style
was included into syllabuses of institutes and *Wu Shu* high-grade
schools.

---

[5] Since 1917 till 1923, before his departure to Hong Kong, Lam Sai Wing
served in the army of *Fujian* province as the Head Instructor in hand-to-hand
combat.

Contents

Iron Thread

***

"This method is the best for those who practice the Martial Arts. I myself could achieve my Tutor *Wong Fei Hung's* results with the use of this method and Master *Fei Hung* could achieve the results of honorable tutor *Lam Fook Sing* who in his time was the best disciple of *Tid Kiu Sam*, the unsurpassed Master..."

Lam Sai Wing

"From my own experience I know that the most impressing thing in *Tid Sin* is that the physical strength of those who practice this method can be increased by nine times. It is hard to believe for those who did not practice this method. Of course, the benefit of *Tid Sin* lies not only in bigger physical strength. The most important thing is robust health and longer life..."

Lei Sai Fai

Foreword

Lei Sai Fai

Tid Sin, or the Iron Thread, is one of the Quan Shu[6] inherited from Tid Kiu Sam[7]. It is a perfect training system aiming at setting into motion body's extremities and the whole body and thanks to it to improve blood circulation and the circulation of the internal energy Qi. Bones, muscles and sinews are subjects of external strengthened, the internal organs and the spirit Shen are subjects of internal strengthened. Therefore, the Spirit and health are improved. A physically weak man becomes a strong one. Besides, those who practice this method can prevent from falling ill with many diseases and live a long life. That's why this method is unsurpassed one among all the methods of Qi Gong and Gong Fu.

---

[6] According to the modern classification the method *Tid Sin* belongs to a branch of "hard", or fighting *Qi Gong*. However, the division of the Martial Arts into *Qi Gong* and *Kung Fu* (or *WU SHU*) is rather conventional in character, it appeared only in the *XX* century as the result of the Western approach to the study of specific oriental phenomenon. Traditionally, *Qi Gong*, or work with the internal energy, was studied in China in the mainstream of general fighting practice, it did not form a separate branch (maybe excepting medical Qi Gong as well as some kinds of religious Qi Gong). Therefore, the author of this article uses Chinese terms *"Quan Shu"* (literally "Art of fist") and *Quan Fa* (literally "Fist technique") in relation to *Tid Sin* in their original wide meaning. In our translation we substituted them for "Qi Gong", a more narrow term that can be understood by a modern reader.

[7] *Tid Kui Sam (in Cantonese)* is translated as *"Iron Bridge III"*, it is a nickname of the great master. His true name was Leung Kwan (1813-1886). He had superhuman strength, hence his nickname (*Jyu Yu Jaai "Short Biography of Master Tid Kui Sam"*).

The founder of the Tid Sin Kuen style is Tid Kiu Sam. In his time he was called one of "Guangdong Ten Tigers". He is a well-known and esteemed person among martial arts masters. Tid Kiu Sam, a favorite disciple of Shaolin monk Gwok Yan, was famous for his mastery, he had no rivals equal to him.

Tid Kiu Sam was on friendly terms with Chen Yi and Xiu Yi Ji, monks from the Haichuang temple[8]. Tid Kiu Sam taught his disciples Choy Jan, Ngau Gi, Ng Hei Goon, Ma Ji Tim, Lam Fook Sing, Si Yiu Leung and some others.

Wong Fei Hung   **Lam Sai Wing**   **Jyu Yu Jaai**
(1847-1924)   **(1860-1943)**

Some time later Lam Fook Sing taught Wong Fei Hung his skills and the latter Wong Fei Hung taught Lam Sai Wing. Lam had about 10,000 disciples, but only a few inherited this secret method – Wu Lap Fung, Pan Gwai Yat, Wai Siu Ba, Chuk Gin Saang, Wong Kai Man, Jeung Sai Biu and my tutor Jyu Yu Jaai, all in all seven men.

---

[8] The *Haichuang Monastery* is situated not far from *Guangzhou*, the administrative center of *Guangdong* province. As a wide-spread legend says, after the famous monastery of Southern Shaolin was burnt to ashes (supposedly in *30-th* of the *XVIII century*) monks who escaped spread in China "like stars in the sky". Few of them found refuge at the *Haichuang Monastery* where they started to teach monks, and later on laymen, the Martial Arts. This monastery is the cradle of the most famous *Kung Fu* styles of the Southern China – *Hung Gar Kuen*, *Fo Kuen*, *Li Gar* and some others.

輝世李

By now[9] my tutor Jyu Yu Jaai passed his skill in the Iron Thread to his son Jyu Ga Yu and his disciples – Wu Jeun Yun (died), Lo Gwai Yik, Tong Hing, Chan Yun Seun (missed during the war), Jung Wai Ming, me and some others.

The Iron Thread is based on twelve secret methods for "arms-bridges" (KIU SAU)[10], each of them corresponds to a certain principle. The "Twelve Bridges" are (Mandarin/Cantonese): GAN/GONG - hardness, steadfastness; ROU/YAU – suppleness, softness; BI/BIK – pressing, coercing, constraining; ZHI/JIK – straightening; FEN/FAN – dividing, separating; DING/DING – steadiness; CUN/CHYUN – quickness, piercing; TIE/TAI – lifting; LIU/LAU – restraining; YIUN/WAN – movement, motion; ZHI/JAI – suppression, subduing; DIN/DING – change, variability.

Besides, it is necessary to keep in mind several factors. Using Qi, or vital force of Spirit, one should be able to increase his physical strength, pay special attention to strengthening his waist and kidneys[11]. Exhalation is done with sounds, it is the external manifestation of such emotions as joy, anger, sorrow and gaiety.

Those are the essentials that make this method different from other kinds of Qi Gong and Gong Fu. I think that the most difficult thing in acquiring Tid Sin is to control your breath and

---

[9] The article was written in 1957.

[10] The term *KIU* ("bridge") in the *Hung Gar* terms means a forearm. There are 12 basic techniques for "forearm-bridges". Those techniques were inherited from the Southern Shaolin. They are also called "*12 Hung's bridges*". Blows with "bridges", i.e. with forearms, is a feature of the Southern Shaolin school.

[11] In accordance with postulates of the Chinese traditional medicine the kidneys are a receptacle of inherent vital energy *Yuan Qi* and a strong and flexible waist is a prerequisite for successful practice in the Martial Arts.

to regulate Qi, to utter sounds and to use the internal exertion. At the same time the above mentioned points are key factors for successful training. A wrong practice can be useless or even harmful. Each kind of Gong Fu has its own method of training and its own secrets. This book just gives the most complete and visual guidance for correct training in Tid Sin. It is indispensable for all who practice Qi Gong and Gong Fu.

From my own experience I know that the most impressing thing in Tid Sin is that the physical strength of those who practice this method can be increased by nine times. It is hard to believe for those who did not practice this method. Of course, the benefit of Tid Sin lies not only in bigger physical strength. The most important thing is robust health and longer life.

Lei Sai Fai

Hong Kong, the summer of Din You year (1957)

Short Biography of Master Tid Kiu Sam

Jyu Yu Jaai

The Shaolin Martial Arts are famous all over the world. Those who inherited them thought that it was the most precious jewel or treasure and seldom left that inheritance to other people. Once a fire broke in the Shaolin temple. The monks dispersed over a wide area. Since that time the Martial Arts of the Shaolin School has started to spread among laymen. It also spread in the province of Guangdong. Those who could get in touch with the Shaolin school of Martial Arts not only comprehensively mastered, but also creatively developed it. Thanks to that fact, step by step, a unique schools was formed. Ten unsurpassed masters called "Ten Tigers from Guangdong" are known among connoisseurs of Martial Arts from the province of Guangdong.

One of them is Tid Kiu Sam. Tid Kiu Sam was born in the town of Nanghai, Guangdong province. He, the third child in the family, became a disciple of a monk from the Shaolin Temple, Gwok Yan. Gwok Yan was one of the greatest masters of the Hung Gar Kuen school. He was known along the whole length of the Yangtse[12] river. Tid Kiu Sam took a serious attitude to training, therefore he perceived the essence of Pugilistic Art. Later on, in connection with training in Martial Arts, he became a follower of Buddhism without taking

---

[12] *Yangtse (Yangtsezhian)*, the longest river in China and Eurasia, flowing from the central part of Tibetan plateau and falling into East China Sea; length: 5,800 km; river basin: 1808.5 thousand km².

monastic vows[13]. His arms were of tremendous power. He could move six sturdy men with his arm, pull them behind himself more than one hundred steps, his features unchanged. The people admired his wonderful strength and called him "Iron Bridge" (Tid Kiu). Meanwhile, his true name was forgotten and he went down to posterity under his nickname Tid Kiu Sam.

Once Tid Kiu Sam, when he was still young and not popular, was invited for a dinner-party. There was a kung fu master, Hu Hai, among the guests. Some guests started to admire talent and abilities of Tid Kiu Sam and asked him to show his strength, but he refused to do so and begged not to mention it. At that moment Hu Hai stood up and challenged him. Tid Kiu Sam politely refused and said: "You are a well-known tutor and I am an ordinary man. For me a victory or a defeat does not mean anything. If I loose, it only means that I need more teaching. It is not so simple for the esteemed master. A defeat will affect your name and position, I kindly ask you to think about it." But Hu Hai insisted and they started to fight. The first attack of Tid Kiu Sam crushed the defense of Hu Hai and achieved the aim. Immediately the second blow followed, it completely depraved Hu Hai the ability to attack and defend himself. Tid Kiu Sam only slightly waved his arm and Hu Hai fell down to the ground, swooned.

---

[13] Besides monks there were so called "ordained novices", or GUIYI DIZI, "reverential followers of Buddha's Doctrine" attached to Buddhist temples. Those were followers of Buddhism who adopted Buddha's Teaching, passed through the ritual of ordainment, had tutors among monks and obtained "secret knowledge". They were laymen and usually did not observe monastic vows. To all appearances, Tid Kiu Sam belonged to this category.

After this incident Hu Hai conceived a hatred for Tid Kiu Sam to the bottom of his heart. Once he met his friend Ma Nan and slandered Tid Kiu Sam. He said, after mastering some methods he, Tid Kiu Sam, looked down at everybody, did not treat the elders with deference and blackened you, Ma Nan. Generally speaking, Ma Nan is a shallow person, they say he is a scarecrow stuffed with straw.

When Ma Nan heard it, he become very angry, sent a man to Tid Kiu Sam at once to make an appointment on the bank of the Haizhu river. Tid Kiu Sam did not understand why Ma Nan had challenged him. He reasoned in such a way: "If I don't accept the challenge, scurrilous gossip about the Shaolin School would be spread, because I am a disciple of the Shaolin School. If I don't attend to this escapade, it would be a disgrace for the whole Shaolin. It would touch my tutors and to disgrace my tutors is worse than death". Not expecting anything good, all the same he accepted the challenge.

At the appointed day and hour Tid Kiu Sam came to the agreed place on the bank of the Haizhu river. Ma Nan saw Tid Kiu Sam come and sent his disciple in a boat to meet him. The disciple said: "Esteemed Tid Kiu Sam, my tutor is waiting for you on board his junk. I kindly ask you to board my boat. My tutor would very glad to meet you". Tid Kiu Sam thought: "Why on board the junk and not on the bank? Probably, it is some trap. By the way, I swim very bad. If I go with him, they will be able to do something to drown me. But I cannot help going. Somehow I should show my capabilities to frighten him". Tid Kiu Sam pretended that he was descending the boat. He put his right foot on the prow and started to press it with all his strength. The prow of the boat started slowly sinking into water. Ma Nan's disciple made a loud exclamation with fright. Tid Kiu Sam removed his foot and said that he was very heavy: "I put only one foot and the boat began to sink. I can not seat in it. I kindly ask to tell your tutor to come to the bank. I shall be waiting for him here". Ma Nan saw everything clearly and understood that the skill of Tid Kiu Sam was higher than his one and he could not rival with him. Ma Nan was frightened and sailed away.

The news of this incident spread very quickly. Tid Kiu Sam's name became famous. After it he measured swords with several distinguished rivals and was the winner every time. His name become even more popular. He was second among "Ten Tigers". Although Tid Kiu Sam did not take monastic vows, he passionately worshipped San Bao[14]. He was associated with a lot of people. Once he got to know monks from the Buddhist temple Haichuang - Chen Yi, Xiu Yi Ji, Zhi Yuan and others. They became his close friends. One of them, Xiu Yi Ji, was in complete command of the Martial Arts and the common interests united them. Their contacts became more frequent. Tid Kiu Sam often spent the night in the temple. Then he met monks from the Baozhi temple where he also spent a lot of time.

At that time a very educated man, Li Cong, lived in the temple. He rented a very small room in the temple and taught children. He was very poor. He was always low in mind, sad and miserable, he coughed and became slim. Tid Kiu Sam felt sorry for him. He taught him a few exercises of the Pugilist Art Tid Sin and told him: "If you regularly practice them, you may cure your cough without any medicine". Li Cong well kept his words in mind and started training in spite of his disease. Only one month passed, but the disease receded. Li Cong was convinced

---

[14] *San Bao* – three treasures of Buddhism: Buddha, his teaching and his followers.

in the efficiency of that method and used it with more diligence. After one year he not only fully recovered, but also improved his health. He continued training.

At that time a monk called Hui Ci lived in the Lingfeng temple. He was a master of the pugilistic fight. He had awfully powerful arms. At one stroke he chopped in two a log with the circumference of seven CUNs[15]. Nobody from the monks around him could vie with him. He was, unlike a Buddhist, hot-tempered and ill-natured, that's why he was called Xie Heshang. Xie means a crab and Heshang means a monk, so it sounds like a crab-monk[16]. The people thought him to be fierce and stubborn and gave him such a nickname. Certainly, it is not a complimentary word, but Hui Ci was satisfied and gladly accepted that nickname.

The temples of Baozhi and Lingfeng were close to each other, therefore Hui Ci often visited the temple of Baozhi at his spare time. He was acquainted with Li Cong. Hui Ci knew that Li Cong was weak and sickly man, but once he saw him sound and strong. He asked: "How did it come?" Li Cong answered: "Recently I have started to practice pugilistic art "The Iron Thread", my body and mind become healthier". Hui Ci said: "You are an educated man, nevertheless you practice the Martial Arts. It is praiseworthy. I also admire this school and kindly ask to give me a few lessons so that I could glorify our temple!" Li Cong politely refused, but Hui Ci, not waiting his consent, started to attack. He suddenly stroke with both fists at the sides

---

[15] 1 *CUN* = ~3.715 cm ~1.463 in

[16] It is common knowledge that the crab goes side-wise. "To go side-wise" in Chinese is " Heng Xing"; it has also another meaning: to spread terror, to commit outrages, to pass all bounds etc.

of Li Cong who did not expect such continuation of their talk. Hui Ci almost achieved his aim.

Fortunately, Li Cong was taught by a well-known master, that's why his response was quicker than that one of an ordinary fighter. He instantly lowered his arms and drew Hui Ci's fists to different sides. The first attack was beaten off, but he immediately used another method - "Hua Long Dian Jing", a blow with fingertips at eyes. Li Cong was astonished: "Why is Hui Ci so ferocious, mean and impudent? He must be taught a good lesson so he would not bully in future!" Li Cong dodged the blow of Hui Ci and delivered a powerful blow at his shin. Hui Ci shouted from surprise and sharp pain and fell down to the ground.

He realized that his skill was not a match to the skill of Li Cong. He folded up his palms and said that it was very instructive. Hui Ci begged to excuse him for his impudence. In his turn Li Cong expressed his regret for not being careful and asked to excuse him for his discourtesy. Hui Ci's leg was seriously injured. There was no bone fracture, but he walked with difficulty. Li Cong helped him to stand up, brought a medicine for injuries and the pain gradually subsided. Hui Ci was very grateful to Li Cong, he asked him: "You have a very high level of mastership. Could you tell me please who taught you?" Li Cong answered: "My tutor's name is Tid Kiu Sam. He still lives in our temple". Hui Ci sadly sighed: " It turned out that such a wonderful talent is near me and I had no idea about it. As the saying goes "one has ears, but cannot hear, another has eyes, but cannot see". Please do not regard me as an impolite man and take me with you. I would like to visit your tutor and get acquainted with such an outstanding master if you don't mind it".

Li Cong complied with his request. Hui Ci limped after Li Cong to Tid Kiu Sam. Certainly, Tid Kiu Sam did not know why Li Cong came to him with that lame man. Li Cong frankly told him what had happened. Tid Kiu Sam reproached him for the imprudent demonstration of his mastership, but Hui Ci took the blame upon himself right away by saying that he was to blame, not Li Cong. "Oh, if it did not happen, I had no chance to meet with the esteemed tutor, - he added. – All my life I took an interest in a wrong branch of Pugilistic Art. Today I have met you and kindly ask you to instruct me. In future I shall not follow blindfold the others!" After Hui Ci said those words he started to make kowtows[17] so vigorously that his forehead swelled. Tid Kiu Sam believed in his sincerity and gave some instructions.

More than a month passed without any fighting methods. Hui Ci was not happy about it and regretted that at one time he had believed Li Cong, he was in low spirits. Hui Ci thought that if he had come to another master, he would have already received something. His disappointment turned to resentment. He suspected that Tid Kiu Sam made a laughing stock of him on purpose. An idea of revenge was ripening in his mind to quench his wrath. He went to Li Er Gong, his former tutor, with the aim to incite him to challenge Tid Kiu Sam. Li Er Gong swallowed the bait.

Hui Ci brought Li Er Gong to Tid Kiu Sam. Tid Kiu Sam saw Hui Ci come with a tall, sturdy man and was ready to greet him. But that man silently looked at him, spit and left. Tid Kiu Sam was puzzled and asked Hui Ci who that man was and why he

---

[17]*Kowtow*, from the Chinese term *Kou Tou* (Cantonese: *Kau Tauh*), lit. "to knock head", the act of kneeling and touching the ground with the forehead to show great deference, submissive respect, etc. formerly made in China.

left without saying a word. Hui Ci said: "He is my former tutor and he came to measure swords with you. Having seen you, he spit and left. I think it is because you are a thin and skinny, while he is in his prime. Such a victory is not worth fighting". Tid Kiu Sam said to that: "Why did your tutor leave me if he wanted to measure swords with me? Now the chance is missed, as he left, but may I see him again?" Hui Ci answered: "Sure, you may!" He ran after Li Er Gong. He overtook him and whispered to him without a tinge of conscience: "Tid Kiu Sam is boasting that his arms, legs and body are like steel ones. If you behave with such self-conceit, he will throw you away at a distance of one XUN[18] in a jiffy". Having heard those words, Li Er Gong become infuriated and immediately returned to measure swords with Tid Kiu Sam. He wanted to knock down Tid Kiu Sam straight off, with one blow. Tid Kiu Sam pretended that he was going to recoil in order to draw him closer, but instead of it he sharply squatted, put his arms round Li Er Gong and threw him on the ground. But Li Er Gong was also a well-trained and strong man. He quickly stood up and started to approach Tid Kiu Sam, trying to deliver a series of blows at his chest. Tid Kiu Sam immediately used the technique BI ZI QUE from the pugilistic art "The Iron Thread" and stopped the enemy's arms. Then he intercepted Li Er Gong's elbow and stroke with his palm at the ribs. Li Er Gong fell down again. He stood up with great effort, staggering, ashamed, and ran away. Tid Kiu Sam beckoned Hui Ci to approach him and said: "I am no longer your tutor and you are not my disciple. Out of my sight, go away!" Hoi Ci left with his head down.

---

[18] *XUN*, a measure of length equal to eight *CHI* (Hong Kong foot, *CHEK* in Cantonese) and one *CHI* is equal to 37.15 cm or 1.219 ft.

Since that time, Tid Kiu Sam made up his mind not to hand down to anybody his unsurpassed Art. However, things always stood so: if you wish to hide something, there are some people who wish to get it. Of course, the case with Tid Kiu Sam who decided not to hand down his mastership was not an exclusion. A rich tradesman named Cai Zan decided to invite Tid Kiu Sam so that he would give lessons on pugilistic art "The Iron Thread" at his home for good money. This offer was accepted by Tid Kiu Sam. Soon a man called Wu Shi Guan from a rich family in the province of Henan also invited Tid Kiu Sam to teach him at his home. He treated him as an honored guest. Then Tid Kiu Sam handed down his skills to one of doctors named Shi Yu Liang and his twin-sons Zhi Tien and Cui Zhu, Lam Fu Cheng and some others. He had small number of disciples and moreover, they did not break their tutor's precepts and handed down their skills to others very seldom. It was believed that the pugilistic art "The Iron Thread" was a precious heirloom of Hung Family (Hung Gar). Those who kept its secrets valued them too high and did not reveal them.

Time, like an arrow, flies quickly. Alas, it does not stop for anybody. Tid Kiu Sam was already past seventy. He lived ether with his pupil Cai or with his pupil Wu. His living conditions were good. Tid Kiu Sam had a lot of spare time at daytime and he formed a bad habit of smoking opium. Bit by bit he addicted to it and consumed more and more opium. Tid Kiu Sam was getting thinner: he stood like a heron with his bones stuck out of his body... However, although Tid Kiu Sam' body was weak, but he was full of daring. Once he heard of a monk named Yi Jie from the Chang temple near the village of Wai Hai who was in full command of the pole technique Wudien Mei Hua Chun[19].

---

[19] *Wu Dien Mei Hua Chun*, lit. "Five Petals of Mume-Plume Blossom"; one of Kung Fu styles, so called "external", or "hard" style which requires good physical conditions.

He could knock out five holes in a wall in a jiffy. Tid Kiu Sam decided to visit him. They met. Yi Jie knew that in Kung Fu circles Tid Kiu Sam was a very known figure. They found common ground at once. Choosing a favorable opportunity, Tid Kiu Sam asked to teach him the art Wudien Mei Hua Chun. Yi Jie said: "You are a famous man in Martial Arts circles. I would be glad to teach you, but you are already in advanced years. Your internal energy has been weakened and moreover, you smoke opium. I dare not teach you because the training requires a high level of lung strain and mainly adjusts breathing. For a physically weak man it is not only useless, but harmful. That's why I beg you to excuse me". But Tid Kiu Sam insisted by saying that he would not leave it at that and master that method. Yi Jie had to teach him.

Yet Yi Jie was right: Tid Kiu Sam had fair age, and moreover, his energy was weakened by opium. His body could not bear such a great load. He had the same daring and aspirations, but to have them is not all: the problem was that he had no enough strength. If you force yourself to train immoderately, you can not attain good results. After all, Tid Kiu Sam fell ill and in ten days or so he could not get up. He died at the age of 73. His disciples buried him at the mountain of Bao Yun Shan, planted trees, made a monument. Since that time the famous Master found eternal rest, but his glorious deeds are not forgotten until the present time.

Meeting with a Nun Good at Martial Arts Reveals Tid Kiu Sam Buddhist Secrets

Jyu Yu Jaai

When people speak about Martial Arts they usually mention Shaolin and set it as an example. Since long ago, for instance, stories about a monk who only with a stick dispersed a big crowd of armed bandits and a lot of other stories like that have been in circulation. Through those stories Shaolin became a well-known and popular place. Traditions of the Temple passed down from generation to generation and spread to the North and the South. During several decades before the fall of the Ming Dynasty (1644) and at the beginning of the rule of the Qing Dynasty, during the years under mottoes of Shun Zhi (1644-1661), Kang Xi (1661-1722) and Qian Long (1736-1796), the development of Martial Arts in Shaolin reached the highest level. At that period growing number of people learned Martial Arts. Members of the Ming imperial family and scions of noble stock could not get used to the thought of the fall of the Imperial House. They were filled with indignation about oppressed state and calamities that fell on the people after the foreign invaders came to power. Many of them were ready to fight courageously for the revival of the nation but under force of circumstances they had to gather strength and expect an opportunity to act. They understood: sitting around and doing nothing, they could become physically and mentally weak and so they started to improve their martial arts skills. Patriots enthusiastically exercised from morning till night, acquired available styles and methods, absorbed all new things, and strove for top mastery. They were ready for hardships and deprivation to attain the only aim: to destroy the enemy and restore the Chinese dynasty of Ming. It was otherwise decreed by fate and the heroes had no chance to fight. However, higher national spirit brought an astounding growth of Shaolin Martial Arts. By mischance, after a little while the Shaolin temple perished in a big fire. Monks who survived, being persecuted by the Qing authorities, dispersed everywhere like stars in the sky. That's how the Shaolin Martial Art got lay society. Some monks set up their own schools. Studies in their sources reveal a common base. Those schools are interconnected like stem, flower and leaves of a lotus: all of them have one root. Their spiritual source is Chan Zong, one of Buddhist schools, and the Shaolin temple is the origin of a whole branch of Martial Arts.

Since long ago the city of Guangzhou has two temples – Guangxiao and Haichuang. Among their numerous monks there were a lot of those who mastered Martial Arts perfectly well. Some of them were consummate masters. Though Tid Kiu Sam[20] did not put up his sophistication in the Martial Art for show and did not flaunt his nick-name "The Iron Kiu", people thought that he knew secrets of Shaolin art. Tid Kiu Sam did not take monastic vows, drank strong drinks and ate meat. All the time he lived at monasteries and did not take the trouble to earn money. If Tid Kiu Sam wished to have a drink but had no money he proposed the following bet: he squats on the brink of

[20] Tid Kiu Sam is translated as "Iron Bridge III"; it was his nick-name, his true name was Leung Kwan (1813-1886).

Lam Sai Wing. Iron Thread. Southern Shaolin Hung Gar Kung Fu Classics Series

齋恩米   Jyu Yu Jaai. Meeting with a Nun Good at Martial
Arts Reveals Tid Kiu Sam Buddhist Secrets

the river and if any man can push him off to water he will lose his nick-name "The Iron Bridge" and allow to call him "The Paper Bridge". Many big guys, seeing a seemingly weakling, thought such a statement to be an empty boast and accepted his challenge. In that case Tid Kiu Sam said: "If you can not push me off to water you ought to spend 100 coins and buy spirits." If somebody agreed to the bet they immediately went to the brink of the river, Tid Kiu Sam squatted at the very edge of water and the man who agreed to bet started to push him. Pushes became stronger and stronger but Tid Kiu Sam never budged. His rival was all of a sweat, his face became red, his breath was heavy, but Tid Kiu Sam was like a tree deeply rooted into the earth: he did not move an inch. So the bet was won. By that time there was a big crowd of gapers around, some thought it was a frame-up and somebody was ready to test his force for 500 coins. Several strong men were chosen and they started to push Tid Kiu Sam; he took the stance SEI PING MA (Horse Stance) and did not budge from his place as if he was cast of metal. With this Tid Kiu Sam charmed everybody and gained general acknowledgement.

As soon as Jing Ming, the monk from the temple Xichan[21], heard about that, he sent a man to invite Tid Kiu Sam. As to Jing Ming, he mastered martial arts and was of a big physical strength. His favorite weapon was an iron stick weighing more than 20 JINs[22]. When monk Jing Ming met Tid Kiu Sam he wanted to check the strength of his legs. The latter said that his legs were as heavy as a mountain. "If I touch the ground only with one toe I become as if rooted deeply into the ground", -

---

[21] **The Xichan Temple is one of the five greatest monasteries in Fujian.**
[22] **10 kg, or 22 lb**

continued Tid Kiu Sam. – "It can be said not only about my legs but my arms that have the same strength as well. If you want to check it, here I am: I am standing with my arm stretched; if somebody can put it down even a little or push me off the place I willingly acknowledge my defeat." At first Jing Ming doubted it but a test showed Tid Kiu Sam's words to be true. Then Jing Ming offered Tid Kiu Sam to accompany him in his travel. The reason was that Jing Ming intended to roam about and collect donations for the renovation of the big statue of Buddha in the temple. He said that he did not feel fear of robbers but one could run into wolves on mountain or forest roads and being alone, without a fellow traveler, it would mean mischief. Jing Ming heard that Tid Kiu Sam belonged to Shaolin School but he was not ready to take a decision if he personally did not make sure of it. He said that this day he was fully convinced in excellent mastery of Tid Kiu Sam and that was why he invited him to collect donations together. Tid Kiu Sam replied with a smile: "Though I did not take monastic vows, my heart belongs to the Temple since long ago. If you do not reject me because of my stupidity I shall join you with pleasure." Jing Ming was very glad to hear it and let Tid Kiu Sam live in the temple.

Several days later Jing Ming and Tid Kiu Sam set out with knapsacks on their backs. They were well treated in all towns and villages on their way. Once, after collection of donations in one of villages, they were about to set out. But the road was strange to them, only fields around, no any buildings at sight; the sun began to set down, just the time before dusk. Suddenly they saw in the distance a temple in the wood. They went without a moment hesitation there. The temple towered over a grove and was surrounded with a high wall. The gate of the temple was set ajar. The yard with bamboos interspaced with pines was seen through a chink in the gate. There were no people there. Birds sang in pine branches, calm and serenity prevailed as if it was another world. The travelers knocked at the gate and waited. A little later a middle-aged nun appeared. She set her hands in a Buddhist greeting and asked; "What can I do for you?" The travelers realized that it was a nunnery. They also set their hands into a greeting, politely asked to be excused and were about to leave. The nun saw that one of the travelers was a monk and the other a layman but both of them set their hands in the greeting, that meant both were followers of Buddha, she reasoned. We all are Buddhists, she said, no excessive formalities are needed among Buddhists; she invited Jing Ming and Tid Kiu Sam to enter the temple. After visiting the sanctuary she led them to the reception room. It should be noted that Tid Kiu Sam was a very sophisticated and experienced in martial arts. He took notice at once that the nun was far from being an ordinary woman. She was lean but she had upright back and sparkling eyes. Light and spring-like steps hinted at strong legs. Tid Kiu Sam knew that it could be achieved only through long and serious training.

Night came. The nun brought some vegetarian food for them. Tid Kiu Sam thanked her and asked if she would be so kind as to say her name under which she is known at the nunnery. "Yun Shen", - the nun answered.

It was quiet in the room where the guest settled for the night. Only one lamp gave dim light, not a slightest sound could be heard. The tired guests fell asleep. In small hours of the night some sound suddenly woke up the travelers. They listened for a while: the sound repeated again and again. Really, something happened? The guests got up and quietly went toward the place from where the sounds were coming. They approached a big hall for praying and saw light there. They cast a cautious glance inside and saw Yun Shen sit in the chair and watch nuns doing exercises. The travelers were in command of martial arts, so it was interesting for them how the nuns did exercises and which school they belonged to. The travelers noiselessly hid in a dark place and watched. Suddenly they heard the voice of Yun Shen: "Why do you stare? You should not look at nuns' training." Jing Ming and Tid Kiu Sam were astonished very much when they heard the voice of the nun: they silently sneaked and hid in the dark place, how could she have noticed them? The friends thought: "No doubt, she has superhuman senses!" They felt uncomfortable. Having left their hiding place, they apologized with respect and said that they had been waken up by yells of her disciples. "We know that such yells accompany exercises but we did not dare to trouble you; that's why we hid in a dark place to watch. We wonder how you saw us. It is quite far from you and it is pitch-dark there to the bargain", - the friends said.

Yun Shen answered with a smile: "I have no special abilities: only my eye and ear are keener than those ones of ordinary people. You trod lightly; the sound of steps was very weak but even that sound I was able to hear. You hid in a dark place but I saw you as distinctly as fire. As you watched for a long time with interest, you seem to be practitioners of martial arts. Will you show us your superb mastery?"

Feeling that nun Yun Shen was an extraordinary woman, they answered that indeed they learned martial arts but their skills were rubbish, not worth looking at. But Yun Shen went on insisting that the guest should show some of their methods and techniques. At last Tid Kiu Sam respectfully put his palms together in front of his breast, then took a low stance and filled his arms and legs with QI. He stood like a mountain. Then he showed some movements from the style "Iron Thread" (Tid Sin) that he mastered to perfection. The demonstration left cracks on the dirt floor where Tid Kiu Sam stood. He thought that the level of his mastery would deserve Yun Shen's praise.

Yun Shen clapped her hands and said: "Your mastery is excellent. You are a worthy follower of the Shaolin School. To reach full perfection, you need a little bit, only two postures – "Tiger's roar" and "Dragon's hissing". Except a small group of people who have access to inmost secrets of Shaolin very few know those postures. They are essential for the direction of QI to arms and hands. The internal force can not be effectively transferred to body extremities without acquiring that technique. Please, do not think that I cavil at trivial, you lack a little bit to reach perfection." On hearing it, Tid Kiu Sam said so: "You have a sagacious and all-seeing eye but my tutor never told me about this methods. Besides, though I am ignorant of those two postures, I do not feel any hindrance to QI flow. Why so?" Yun Shen replied to it: "You yourself know that it is hard to believe words without facts. The nuns also can do what you have showed. All of us are followers of Buddha, we discuss together existing problems and try to find right solutions. It is a good matter, it does not lead to confrontation. I shall tell the youngest nun to compete with you. You will have a few rounds. She knows the postures "Tiger's roar" and "Dragon's hissing" and you don't. Let facts show who is right."

Tid Kiu Sam wished to prove the correctness of his words, he joined his palms before his breast as a sign of respect and said: "I am grateful to you for your just words and ready for a test." Yun Shen beckoned one of the nuns and told her to contest with Tid Kiu Sam. As soon as rivals approached, Tid Kiu Sam immediately felt that the nun's arm is as heavy as a mountain: all his strength will not be enough to overwhelm her. Several times, using various methods and techniques, Tid Kiu Sam attacked the nun but all his attacks failed. At the height of fighting Yun

Shen suddenly cried: "Stop!" Tid Kiu Sam and the nun stopped fighting. Yun Shen asked Tid Kiu Sam: "I was right, was not I?" Tid Kiu Sam exclaimed: "My gentle teacher, I did not know that there are still gaps in my education!" Yun Shen replied to it: "You already know what you lack but you do not know how to replenish it, therefore you will not be able to get full success. I want to help you." She explained to Tid Kiu Sam essentials of techniques unknown to him and showed how to exercise them.

Then Yun Shen said such words: "Buddha's teaching is based on clemency and virtue. I never heard that the aim of training is to surpass others. If you exercise under pretext of self-defense but keep aggressive thoughts against others in your mind, those thoughts are sinful. Sinful thoughts lead into temptation and illusions. It contradicts the very idea of Buddhism. Since the time when Bodhidharma taught Buddhist monks secret training methods laymen considered temples nothing else than cloisters of martial arts. But that is nonsense. Methods of training of physical body is only an initial stage. The aim of Buddhism is to reach Nirvana to cognize Truth. But this task is too great for our temple. We have mastered the whole complex of methods to acquire Gong Fu. There are few among learners of martial art who honor "Three Treasures"[23] of Buddhism. The most people are eager to get only strength and mastery. But recall Xian Yu[24] with his superhuman huge force who alone could withstand ten thousands of warriors; after all, he committed suicide. Since you came here, it would be inappropriate to let you go empty-

[23]"Three Treasures of Buddhism" (San Bao) – Buddha, his teaching and his disciples.

[24] An outstanding military leader of the principality of Chu. In 206 B.C. Xian Yu usurped power and declared himself the Grand Duke of the Western Chu. In 202 B.C. the army of Xian Yu was defeated by Emperor's superior forces in a battle near Gaixia. Xian Yu surrounded by enemies committed suicide.

齊恩米

handed. I want you to escape nets of illusions and delusions and take the right way, let the Buddhist idea find its place in your martial art. If you follow this principle it will not be difficult to reach the top mastery. If you neglect this it will be impossible to become a follower of the orthodox school even if you have acquired good mastery."

Tid Kiu Sam heartily thanked the nun. In future he became a famous master.

IRON THREAD

 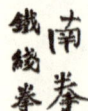

GING LAI HOI KYUN
1. A Greeting Before the Beginning

Raise your hands and join them in a greeting. The right hand is clenched into fist, the left hand is an opened palm, like shown in the picture (Fig.1). The right leg is slightly bent in the knee and the left foot advances, you assume the stance DUI MA[25]. Left foot touches the ground only with its toe. You stare to the south. Breathe in deeply through slightly opened lips ("to take Qi") and hold your breath with some effort ("to close Qi"). Then clench your fists and turn your hands with the centers of the palms up, return the left foot to the right one and draw your hands to the waist. Stand upright, straighten both legs. You assume the position YI FU CHIM JUNG - "Two Tigers Hide Their Traces" (Fig.2).

---

[25] *DUI MA* (in Cantonese), *DIAO MA* or *MA DIAO JIAO* (in Mandarin) – literally, "A Hanging Stance" or "A Stance with a Hanging Foot", the stance in which the main weight of the body rests on one (rear) leg, another (front) leg only slightly touches the ground with its toe; it is also known as "Cat's Stance".

第 一 式

敬 禮 開 拳

鐵 綫 拳

Fig.1

Lam Sai Wing. IRON THREAD.
Southern Shaolin Hung Gar Kung Fu Classics Series

林世榮

鐵線拳 南拳

YI FU CHIM JUNG
2. Two Tigers Cover Up Their Traces

From the first position GING LAI – "A Greeting Before the Beginning" continue the execution. Clench your hands into fists, turn the fists before your breast with the centers of palms back, draw both fists to the waist and turn them with the centers of palms upward. Do not stick out your chest, do not raise your shoulders, look straight forward, both legs are straight, stand firmly. Pay attention to concentration of force LI in both thighs, the head is as if a cap weighing 1000 JINs26 lies on it. The mouth is closed, breathe in and breathe out through the nose three times, maintain stable and strong posture. Then arms will do the next movement.

Comments: After a greeting gesture (**Fig.1**) clench your left hand into fist with force, turn the fists with the centers of palms toward you and pull them to your waist. Simultaneously with hand movements the left leg is moved back to the right one. It is position YI FU CHIM JUNG – "Two Tigers cover up their traces": the fists are on the sides of the waist, their back sides faces the ground, the feet are in parallel with each other, the distance between them is about one fist (**Fig.2**).

Requirements to the coordination of different body parts are as follows: the shoulders are lowered and slightly moved forward, the breast is slightly bent inward, the diaphragm is in its lower position (that corresponds to "stomach" breathing),

---

[26] **1000 JINs are approximately equal to 500 kg, or 1100 lb (a figure of speech).**

第 二 式

二 虎 潛 踪

鐵 綫 拳

Fig.2

the stomach is strained and "filled", the hands are tightly clenched into fists. The tongue should touch upper palate, the mouth is closed, the teeth are clenched without effort, the chin is slightly drawn in, the look is strictly forward. If you imagine vividly enough that you carry some weight on your head, the position of your head, neck and upper part of spine would adjust themselves correspondingly. The lower part of the body: the thighs are strained, the buttocks are "pulled in", the pelvis is put slightly forward and upward, due to it the lower part of the spine is straightened and is on one vertical line with the upper part of spine and the neck. The knees are straightened, but not completely. Try to "cling" to the ground with your toes (however, do not bend them), it helps "to take root". At the start it demands some conscious efforts, but after some practice you will take the right posture automatically.

In this position breathe in and breathe out three times, at this time your fists are moved back and down at the level of the coccyx. The fists are moved through three stages when you breathe out, they are immovable when you breathe in. The movement is executed slowly and with some effort: just imagine that you try to bend a thick iron wire. At the end of the third exhalation you take **position 2**: your fists are clenched with effort, your wrists are bent towards the inner side of the forearm, the elbows are directed backward (**Fig.2**). All the above requirements to the stance are maintained.

SEUNG GIM CHAI KIU
3. Bridges Hacking Like Pair of Swords[27]

A straight stance as shown in the previous picture (Fig.2). Both fists are "pulled up" from behind, moved forward along the sides of the ribs and reach the position under armpits; then the fists (with palm centers) turn to face each other, unclench and form the position CHAI JEUNG – "The cutting palms". At this moment you should open your mouth and breathe out, after it the "cutting palms" move forward very slowly and arms stretch. You should breathe out and utter "HO-O".

Comments: When you are in previous position YI FU CHIM JUNG (**Fig.2**) make a deep breath through the nose. With that the breast is slightly raised up without sticking out, the shoulders remain lowered. During inhalation the fists move up and at the end of inhalation they are on the sides of ribs under the armpits, the back of the hand down. Then fists are transformed to CHAI JEUNG – "Cutting palms" and do a short push forward at the breast level. That phase of the movement is shown in the picture for this position: the arms are bent, the elbows are lowered, the distance between the palms and the breast is from 20 to 25 cm (**Fig.3**). Simultaneously with the palms push, do a short breath-out from the upper part of the lungs through the mouth with uttering the sound "**HO-O**"; at the same time the abdomen remains strained and "filled". Without stopping in this position the arms start slowly

---

[27] The term "Bridge" (*KIU*) in the Hung Gar terms means a forearm. There are 12 basic techniques for "forearm-bridges". Those techniques were inherited from the Southern Shaolin. They are also called "12 Hung's bridges".

 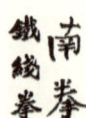

straightening forward, the movement is executed with some effort and with gradual exhalation through the nose. At the end of the movement another short push is executed with breath-out through the mouth with the sound "**HO-O**"[28]. In the final phase the arms are slightly bent in the elbows, the elbows are turned downward.

Explanation: During this exercise just imagine that you are standing close to a very big and heavy iron ball that you must push as far as possible. At the first moment you should gather yourself up and move the ball from its place, then you gradually, with constant effort, straighten your arms and accelerate the ball, at the end you give it a certain momentum with a push. At the external level this piece of imagination allows you to attain the right coordination of breathing with the work of muscles and sinews and at the internal level to unite the force-Li with breath-Qi. At the initial stage of training mental concentration has uttermost importance, it is called *"The Thought Leads Qi"* in the tradition of the Shaolin QiGONG. After some practice any of your movements will be filled with the internal energy Qi without any effort of your consciousness. That is the final aim of Shaolin QiGONG practice. Shaolin treatises on pugilism say: *"When each movement of your body is fused with the breath-Qi, your arms and legs become quick and strong like those ones of a monkey. So the man moves like a lightning in the sky and joyfully he passes along as a victor in all battles."* /De Chang. Shaolin Qi Gong. Zhangzhou, 1983/

---

[28] In this *TAOLU* several types of breathing are used, each type relates to a certain action at the "external" level and reinforces it according to the principle *"The Force-Li Comes With the Breath-Qi"*. A sound uttered during exhalation is a manifestation of the "internal" effort and comes as if from the stomach (from the region *DANTIAN*), therefore one should not simulate it artificially. At first it is better to concentrate on the coordination of motion and breathing.

第 三 式

雙 劍 切 橋

鐵 線 拳

六

Fig3.

LOU JANG TIU DAAN
4. Venerable Monk Carries a Yoke

You are standing in a straight position as shown in the previous picture (Fig.3). Your palms shoulder-width apart with fingers pointed upward. Turn your hands (with fingers) down and the centers (of the palms) upward. Then "divide three joints" (bend an arms in shoulder, elbow and wrist joints), clench your fists and pull them up. Both elbows move away from the side ribs, facing down as before; both forearms keep vertical-diagonal position. Both fists are "pulled up", reach the level of cheeks and stop. During that movement you straighten your chest and breathe out with uttering the sound "H-E".

Comments: From the previous position (arms are stretched forward at the shoulder level, palm centers face each other) rotate the palms in the wrist joints – left hand counter-clockwise, the right hand clockwise to turn palm centers upward (with this the fingers are directed forward and downward). At the time of rotation the wrist joints must be strained and bent in the extreme in the direction of the outer side of a forearm. Then slowly and with some effort clench the hands into fists with simultaneous bending the wrists toward the inner side of the forearm and pull the fists to the shoulders. This movement is slow and strained as if you pull toward you a heavy thing. Those actions are done with a slow and deep breath-in through the nose. After a small pause raise up your fists at the cheek level and pull them apart to take the position "Venerable monk carries a yoke". The movement is carried out at a middle speed. Just imagine that you are in a narrow corridor and try to move aside the walls with your forearms; in the final stage the effort reaches maximum and it is accompanied by a short breath out with uttering the sound "**H-E**" through the mouth (the lips are

lightly parted, the teeth are clenched, as if you "spit out" some air from the upper part of your lungs).

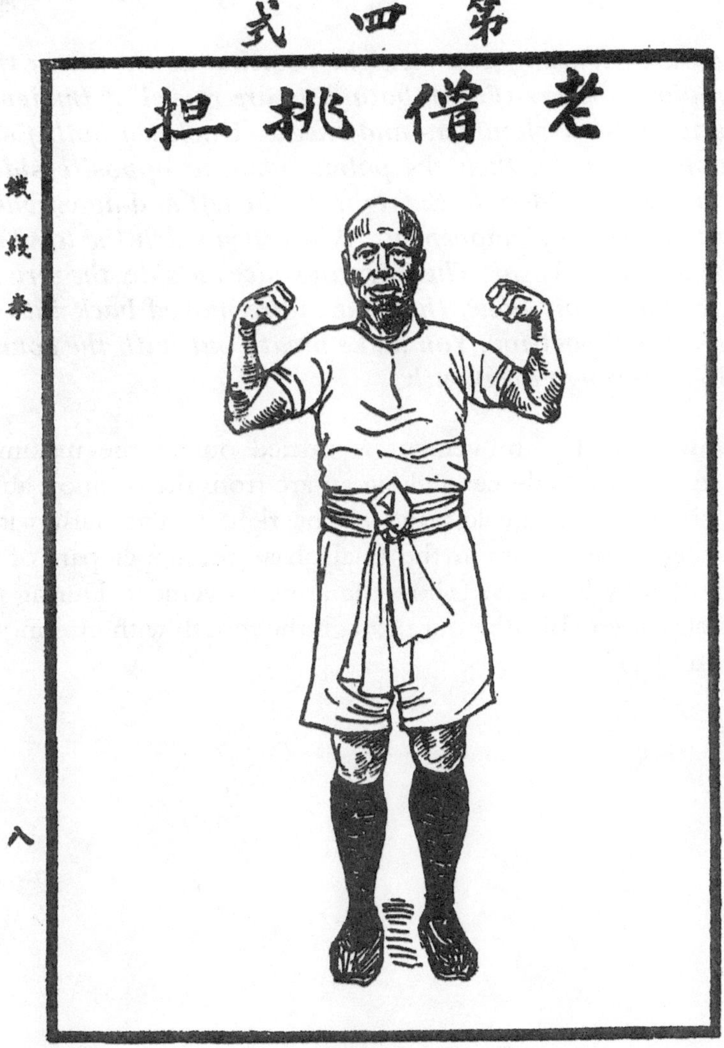

Fig.4

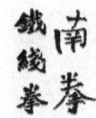

Lam Sai Wing. IRON THREAD.
Southern Shaolin Hung Gar Kung Fu Classics Series

GING NGAAN LIN YIK
5. A Frightened Goose Flaps Its Wings

You are standing in a straight position as shown in the previous picture (Fig.4), both fists are raised at the level between your shoulders and cheeks. Unclench both fists simultaneously, then the palms move to opposite sides from the shoulders to the right, to the left and downward with a "cutting" movement. When they reach the level of the waist they stop. The fingertips face outside, the wrists butt the pelvic bone, the elbows are moved back into a "prop-up" position. You make breath out with the sound "H-E" through the mouth.

Comments: The movement is carried out at the maximum speed, the palms descend along an arc from the position above the shoulders to the left and to the right to the waist with a "cutting" movement. In the final phase the upper part of the body slightly bends to follow the arms movement. During that movement you breathe out through the mouth with uttering the sound "**H-E**".

第 五 式

驚 鴻 飲 翼

鐵 線 拳

—○—

Fig.5

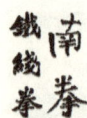
JO YAU CHYUN KIU
6. Piercing Bridges[29] to the Left and to the Right

The position of the torso is straight. Both palms from the position on the waist are pulled apart at the same time, the arms are stretched to the right and to the left. After reaching the shoulder level and locating on one line they stop; at the same time the thorax expands. The movement is made with an exhalation through the mouth and with uttering "CHI".

Comments: From the previous position (**Fig.5**) deliver piercing blows to the right and to the left with finger tips as shown in the picture (**Fig.6**). The movement is made as quick as possible, the fingers are straight and strained. Imagine that there are paper screens on your left and on your right and you need to pierce small holes. During that movement you breathe out through the clenched teeth with uttering the sound "**CHI**".

---

[29] The term *KIU* ("bridge") in the *Hung Gar* terms means a forearm. There are 12 basic techniques for "forearm-bridges". Those techniques were inherited from the Southern Shaolin. They are also called "12 Hung's bridges". *CHYUN KIU* is one of 12 "bridge techniques". In fact, it is a quick strike with finger tips of an open palm.

第 六 式

左 右 寸 橋

Fig.6

SAAM DUK JYU KIU
7. Build the Pearl Bridge Thrice

The position of the torso is straight, your shoulders and your arms form a straight line. Then your left and right arms slightly descend, both palms turn to the position JYU KIU – "Pearl Bridge". You strain the thorax and at once both "Pearl Bridges" very slowly pull to the shoulders and take place between your shoulders and ears. Utter "S-I", at the same time "Pearl Bridges" are slowly stretched to the left and to the right. The movement is made three times.

Comments: After delivering blows to sides bend your wrists toward the outer side of the forearms, at the same time change the position of your hands according to the picture (**Fig.7**). The arms are slightly bent in elbows, the elbows and the wrists slightly descend ("sink" in the original text). The movement is fast as if you jerk your hands slightly down and toward you (however, the amplitude of the movement is small, you only slightly bend your arms in elbows). Requirements to hand position: your forefingers are completely straightened and directed upward, other fingers are bent and pressed to the edge of the palm, palm centers are directed to sides; the wrists are bent in the extreme and with effort, you should feel some tension in fingers, palms and wrists. Slightly spread your fingers in this position: the tension in the sinews will grow. Then slowly pull your hands to the shoulders, at the same time you breathe in through the nose. That phase of the movement is shown in the picture (**Fig.7**). After it draw your palms to both sides at the shoulder level slowly, with some effort. The movement is made together with breath out through slightly parted lips and a low hissing sound "**S-I**". Imagine that you try to move apart cliffs in a narrow cleft. Then while breathing in, slowly pull "The Pearl

bridges" to your shoulders. Execute it three times. **Be careful with this exercise: do not strain yourself extremely, if you have higher blood pressure.**

第 七 式

三 度 珠 橋

鐵 綫 拳

一四

Fig.7

 Lam Sai Wing. IRON THREAD.
Southern Shaolin Hung Gar Kung Fu Classics Series

DAAI SIN GUNG SAU
8. Great Immortal Raises His Hands in Greeting Gesture

The position of the body is straight and upright. The "Pearl Bridge" of the right arm transforms: the hand clenches into fist. The "Pearl Bridge" of the left arm also transforms: the hand is in the position "palm". After it the right fist and the left palm simultaneously and very slowly move forward and draw together but the left palm is a little ahead of the right fist. Then the left palm clenches into fist and both fists descend along the torso and move back, as if you are pulling something toward you. The movement is made without sound exhalation.

Comments: After the execution of the previous exercise three times, clench your right hand into fist and transform the left hand into the position "palm": all fingers except the thumb are straight. Then both arms stretch forward and you take position DAAI SIN GUNG SAU - "Great Immortal Raises His Hands in Greeting Gesture" (**Fig.8**). The movement is made slowly and with some effort, exhalation is soundless, through the nose. Then, clench the left palm into fist and slowly draw both fists to your waist. In that way you take position YI FU CHIM JUNG - "Two Tigers Cover Up Their Traces" (**Fig.2**). This movement is accompanied by a deep and a long-drawn inhalation through the nose. Do not forget about mental concentration on the movement: imagine that your hands are bending a thick iron wire with its ends wound on your fists.

第 八 式

大 仙 拱 手

鐵 線 拳

一 六

Fig.8

Lam Sai Wing. IRON THREAD.
Southern Shaolin Hung Gar Kung Fu Classics Series

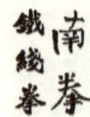

YI JI KIM YEUNG MA
9. Straddle the Beam with Pincers-Shaped Legs in the Stance of Hieroglyph "YI" (二)

The position of the body is straight and upright. From the position in front of your chest both fists are already pulled to you and drawn back. Stand on tiptoe, at the same time raise your heels up and bring them apart with a twisting movement. After your heels touch the ground, the tiptoes are raised and turned. Thus, the feet are being parted to the left and to the right. When the distance between the feet becomes 1 CHEK and 2 CHYUNs[30] they stop. After it the body "settles down" (descends a little), both knees are slightly bent, the thighs are open outside, the force LIK concentrates in the shins, thus a "Pincers-Shaped" stance is formed. The movement is made without sound exhalation.

Comments: Position 9 differs from **position 2** only in feet position. It is necessary to pay special attention to the position of your shins: they must be strictly vertical, the knees are not drawn inside. Imagine that you tightly grapple a beam of square cross-section with your knees and shins, the side of the beam is about the length of your shin (about 45-50 cm or a little longer, depending on your height). Your knees are bent a little, your feet are parallel, the toes should "cling" to the ground (however,

---

[30] **The distance between the feet is about 45 cm, or 1,5 ft.**

第 九 式

二字拑陽馬

鐵線拳

一八

Fig.9

don't bend your toes, the soles should be tightly pressed to the ground). The inner side of your thighs and shins should feel some strain, moreover you should feel twisting tension in your shins. At the same time the requirements contained in the comments on **position 2** are applied to the upper part of the body, don't forget about it. Moving feet apart is done during an exhalation (**Fig.9**).

YIM WU DAANTIN
10. Cover DAANTIN[31]

Stance YI JI KIM YEUNG MA (Fig.9). The mouth is tightly closed, you breathe out through your nose and utter "M-M". Both fists go out from your back, the right fist is below the left fist, the left forearm presses (from above) to the right forearm, as if you "cut" forward (with your forearms) in a crossed position. Cover DAANTIN with your forearms and take the defensive position YIM WU.

Comments: When you are in previous position (**Fig.9**), quickly breathe in through your nose. Then, your arms move from behind your waist forward to position before your abdomen, at the same time you make a short strained exhalation of a small amount of the air from the upper parts of the lungs (due to lowering a thorax). The movement is made with an increasing effort; the mouth is closed, the teeth are clenched, the tongue is raised to the upper palate, exhalation is made through the nose. The amount of exhaled air is controlled with muscles of the throat and vocal cords, due to it a higher pressure is built up in the abdominal cavity compressed with muscles of diaphragm, abdomen and waist. At that time you utter "**M-M**". In the final stage of the movement you interrupt the sound: the air is blocked (by the muscles of the throat) and the pressure in the abdomen (and accordingly in the region of DAANTIN) increases. At the external level it corresponds to the moment of the highest tension of muscles and sinews in the whole body:

---

[31] *DAANTIN* (in Cantonese), literally "cinnabar field", the same as *DANTIAN* in Mandarin.

you must have a feeling of being a rock deeply rooted in the earth. This maximum tension with stopped breathing lasts about 1 second. Requirements to the stance: the stomach is "filled", strained and slightly stuck out forward, the backbone is slightly arched outside in contrast to the thorax which is arched inside. Muscles and sinews of the whole body toughen; however, the main effort is concentrated in your arms and the lower part of the stomach.

The stopped breathing after inhalation accompanied by muscle and mental strain is a very effective means for the development of extraordinary capabilities of a human body. However, it is a drastic means, its wrong use can lead to dangerous consequences. If you have some problems with your health, you should see your doctor before starting to train. At any rate, you should not strain yourself too much at the beginning. At first, you should catch the "inner" sense of the movement and only after that make muscular efforts. Carefully analyze your feelings. When you feel that your body has got stronger, increase loads step by step.

第 十 式

掩 護 丹 田

Fig.10

Lam Sai Wing. IRON THREAD.
Southern Shaolin Hung Gar Kung Fu Classics Series

JAU SAU WU HUNG
11. Raise Up Arms and Cover Breast

You are in the previous position (Fig.10). Your feet firmly stand in the stance YI JI KIM YEUNG MA - "Straddle the Beam with Pincers-Shaped Legs in the Stance of Hieroglyph YI". At first, open your mouth and remove "muddy air", an exhalation is accompanied by a sound "H-O". After it, bend your elbows and raise up your arms. The right fist, hooked inside, is outside; the left fist is inside and presses forward (i.e. the left forearm presses on the right one). Both fists simultaneously pull upward, reach the level of the throat and stop.

Comments: After the execution of the previous exercise, relax your muscles (but not completely; muscles, especially muscles of abdomen, hands and forearms, retain some tension). At the same time breathe out through the mouth with a sound "H-O". Then your hands move up at the level of your throat. The movement is executed slowly and with some effort. At the same time breathe in through the nose. Observe that your fists should be tightly clenched, wrists should be bent towards the inner side of your forearm, the forearms should press each other. Get a feeling of some tension in your arms.

十 一 式

抽 手 護 胸

鐵 經 拳

二 二

Fig.11

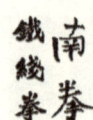

LEUNG SAU JE TIN
12. Shield the Sky with Both Hands

Like the previous position, feet are in the stance YI JI KIM YEUNG MA - "Straddle the Beam with Pincers-Shaped Legs in the Stance of Hieroglyph YI". The air reaches the mouth and goes out with a sound "YEU". You concentrate force between your elbow joints, your fists are half-unclenched, the left hand from inside presses on the right forearm, the right hand are bending inside, a crossed position of the hands is formed. Raise your hands to the level of the forehead and stop there.

Comments: The expression "to concentrate force between your elbow joints" seems to mean that it is necessary to move your elbows inside with some effort. Then the fists are transformed into the position "Tiger's claws" and your hands are jerked up with force. At the same time your knees slightly bend and the torso descends a little. Those actions are accompanied by a short breath out through the mouth with uttering the sound "**YEU**".

十 二 式
兩 手 遮 天

鐵 綫 拳

二 四

Fig.12

CHEUN CHUNG HIN GIM
13. Cheun Chung Hands a Sword

Position YI JI KIM YEUNG MA - "Straddle the Beam with Pincers-Shaped Legs in the Stance of Hieroglyph YI". Force is concentrated in both elbows and between elbows, both hands descend from the forehead down, your mouth utters a sound "HEI". The downward movement of your elbows is accompanied by an exhalation.

Comments: It is a fast and strong movement, your elbows with some effort are brought inward, as if you squeeze between them some thing, your forearms are vertical. Besides, this movement has an applied meaning; by the way, many other movements also have an applied meaning in this TAOLU, as TID SIN is a combat style. If the enemy has caught you for your throat or your clothes, free yourself from his lock with a strong elbow blow from up to downward at his forearms. During that movement you breathe out through the clenched teeth with uttering the sound "**HEI**".

十 三 式

秦 琼 献 鐧

鐵 線 拳

二 六

Fig.13

NGO YING POK SIK
14. The Hungry Falcon Swoops Down on Its Prey

You firmly stand in the stance YI JI KIM YEUNG MA - "Straddle the Beam with Pincers-Shaped Legs in the Stance of Hieroglyph YI". At first, from the position YI JI KIM YEUNG MA you pass to a low stance SEI PING DAAI MA[32], immediately after it you bend your waist and stoop forward, raise up your head, your eyes stare straight forward. Both arms are brought apart to the left and to the right like spread wings of a bird. The movement is soundless.

Comments: Thighs in the stance NGO YING POK SIK are in parallel with the ground, back is slightly concave, shoulder-blades are brought together, but it is done without big effort, the crown of your head is directed up, eyes stare straight forward and far off. In the process of taking the stance a deep breathing in through the nose is being made.

---

[32] *SEI PING DAAI MA* – literally, "four level stance of a big horse", i.e. a low firm stance.

十四式

餓鷹撲食

鐵線拳

二八

Fig.14

Lam Sai Wing. IRON THREAD.
Southern Shaolin Hung Gar Kung Fu Classics Series

BAAK KIU
15. Push with Bridges

From the low position SEI PING DAAI MA the whole body raises up. In such a way you pass on from the low stance SEI PING DAAI MA to the vertical stance YI JI KIM YEUNG MA ("Straddle the Beam with Pincers-Shaped Legs in the Stance of Hieroglyph YI"). The elbows of both arms "sink" (i.e. turn downward), the hands moves up toward your breast on the left and on the right. The position BAAK KUI –"Push with bridges" is formed. Utter a sound "E-I" simultaneously with the arms movement.

Comments: Being in the previous position (**Fig.14**), turn your elbows down, the hands with fingers upward. Then, simultaneously with straightening your body, your hands move along an arc toward the breast and upward. This movement is powerful and quick, work of your legs, torso and arms is coordinated, as if you make a push with your palms from down upward, using the force of arms, legs and waist. In the final stage of the movement you utter a cry "**E-I**".

十 迫

式 五 橋

峨 縱 拳

三

〇

Fig.15

DING GAM KIU
16. A Stable Gold Bridge

Feet are in the position YI JI KIM YEUNG MA ("Straddle the Beam with Pincers-Shaped Legs in the Stance of Hieroglyph YI"). Force is concentrated in the thumbs of both hands and in the both wrists. Both palms move forward with a pushing movement (TEUI). The movement of the arms is accompanied by a sound "HO-O". You stare ahead.

Comments: From the previous position (**Fig.15**), draw your elbows a little back and turn hands with the centers of palms forward at the shoulder level. At the same time, change the position of your hands to the following position: four of your fingers are completely straight and spread wide with effort, the thumb is perpendicular to the palm plane and directed forward. Your wrists are bent toward the outer side of your forearms. You should feel some tension in wrists and thumbs. Then, slowly and with some effort stretch your arms and take the position "A Stable Gold Bridge" (**Fig.16**). Straightening of arms is accompanied by a low and prolonged expiration with a sound **"HO-O"** through slightly opened mouth. Here and further, the above requirements to the stance YI JI KIM YEUNG MA are valid, remember about it (see comments to **Position 9**).

十六式

定金橋

Fig.16

Lam Sai Wing. IRON THREAD.
Southern Shaolin Hung Gar Kung Fu Classics Series

FU HAAU LUNG YAM
17. Roar of the Tiger and Twitter of the Dragon

From the stance YI JI KIM YEUNG MA ("Straddle the Beam with Pincers-Shaped Legs in the Stance of Hieroglyph YI") turn outside the toes of both feet a little, immediately descend the upper part of your body, in this way pass from the stance YI JI KIM YEUNG MA to the stance SEI PING BAAT FAN MA. At the same time, raise your elbows forward, the palms of both hands turn upward and move to position above your shoulders and below the level of the ears. Shake with your palms many times. The movement of the palms is accompanied by a sound "E-E-E". You stare ahead.

Comments: From the previous position (**Fig.16**), descend into the low stance SEI PING BAAT FAN MA[33]. Immediately after that your arms are bent in elbows, you take the position shown in the picture (**Fig.17**). Then, shake your hands above your shoulders quickly, as if a "gust of the wind swings a willow". Simultaneously with the arms movement, you make a long strenuous breath out through your mouth. At that moment your teeth are almost clenched, your lips are stretched, the position of the tongue and the vocal chords corresponds to the position when one pronounces the sound "**E-E**" (as in "bed"), but due to a strong thrust of expired air the sound is like rather something between whistle and hiss.

---

[33] *SEI PING BAAT FAN MA*, literally, "four level and eight parts horse stance", i.e. a low firm stance.

十七式

虎嘯龍吟

鐵線拳

三四

Fig.17

 *Lam Sai Wing. IRON THREAD.*
Southern Shaolin Hung Gar Kung Fu Classics Series

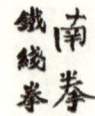

SEUNG CHYUN KIU
18. A Pair of Piercing Bridges

The toes of both feet in the stance SEI PING BAAT FAN MA turn a little inside, the upper part of the body raises up, in such a way you return from the stance SEI PING BAAT FAN MA to the stance YI JI KIM YEUNG MA ("Straddle the Beam with Pincers-Shaped Legs in the Stance of Hieroglyph YI"). Both palms rush forward from the breast with a "clap"[34] – it is a straight blow BIU[35]. The movement is accompanied by a sound "E-I".

Comments: After the execution of the previous exercise you pull your hands to the breast with a jerk and immediately deliver a fast piercing blow forward with finger tips of an open palm. At the same time the legs are straightened, you take the stance YI JI KIM YEUNG MA. The moment of delivering the blow coincides with the moment of coming into the stance. Note that your arms in elbow joints do not straighten completely or to the full extent, they keep a hardly visible bent position: "arms are straight and not straight, bent and not bent". A shout "**E-I**" coincides with the concentration of a piercing effort in the final stage of this movement: imagine that you should thrust your fingers into tough elastic substance as deep as possible. Requirements to hands position: four fingers are completely straight, pressed to each other with some effort, the thumb is bent and pressed to the edge of the palm.

---

[34] A clap made by sleeves of your clothes, while performing this quick movement.
[35] *BIU CHYUN*, "piercing blow", a blow with ends of fingers of an open palm.

十 八 式
雙 寸 橋 

Fig.18

JAI KIU

19. Overpowering Bridges

The stance YI JI KIM YEUNG MA ("Straddle the Beam with Pincers-Shaped Legs in the Stance of Hieroglyph YI"). Both palms return to the position lower than the ears, you separate three joints and after it clench your fists. Then, both fists move forward and obliquely downward very slowly. The movement is accompanied by a sound "E-I", you look ahead.

Comments: After delivering a double blow BIU your hands return to the position above your shoulders to the level a little lower than your ears. However, this time the centers of your palms are directed forward, elbows are drawn to both sides and a little back, all fingers are straight with some effort and spread wide. Make a breath-in through the nose at the same time. Then, lower your hands to your breast and at the same time clench them into fists with a catching movement. Without stopping the movement, slowly and with some effort, lower your arms to both sides and a little forward and take the position JAI KIU (**Fig.19**). The effort is directed to outside and downward. At the end of the movement the strain of muscles of your whole body reaches maximum and is accompanied by a shout "**E-I**". Do not forget: the sound must come out from your "belly". Actually it means a strong contraction of stomach muscles. However, the abdomen does not pull in and remains "filled" and a little protruded. Thus, the sound is manifestation of higher pressure inside the abdominal cavity.

十 九 式

制

橋

蠍鍛拳

三

入

Fig.19

FAN GAM CHEUI
20. A Blow Dividing Gold

The stance YI JI KIM YEUNG MA ("Straddle the Beam with Pincers-Shaped Legs in the Stance of Hieroglyph YI"). At first, both fists from the position below and on both sides are pulled and returned back to your chest. The right arm is outside, the left one is inside, the forearms form a crossed position. Your mouth is closed, you breathe out through the nose with a sound "M-M", at the same time your fists are parted to both sides with a "splitting" movement. You stare ahead.

Comments: Bend your arms and cross your forearms before your breast. From this position your fists move slightly upward and to both sides and then downward in the vertical plane. The fists are tightly clenched, wrists bent to the inner side of the forearm, forearms strained. The arms movements are accompanied by an expiration through the nose with a sound "M-M". The coordination of breath and muscle force completely corresponds to **Position 10** (see comments). The only difference is that in this case the force is directed to both sides and downward. Requirements to the stance are also similar.

式 十 二
趙 金 分

鐵 綫 拳

〇 四

Fig.20

YI FU CHIM JUNG
21. Two Tigers Cover Up Their Traces

Your feet are in the position YI JI KIM YEUNG MA. According to position 9 where the method of taking the stance is described, you turn your heels and toes in a reverse sequence and draw your feet together. That movement is made in three stages, you draw feet together and take an upright position. At the same time both fists are also pulled to you and moved back in three movements. After the fists have been moved back, you utter a sound "H-O" to breathe out muddy air.

Comments: Shift body weight to the heels and turn your feet with its toes inside. Then tiptoe and bring together the heels. With the third movement place your feet parallel each other. The distance between the feet is equal to the width of a fist. At the same time pull your fists to the torso and then back to the waist. In this case requirements to the stance completely coincide with the requirements given in comments on **Position 2**. The expiration with a sound **"H-O"** is made through the mouth.

世 一 廿

二 庚 潛 踪

式

鐵
綫
拳

二
四

Fig.21

SIN MIN JI NG

22. Open out a Fan in the Stance JI NG

From the previous position (Fig.21), make a step with your left leg to the left and turn the toe of the right foot a little to the right, thus the position JI NG MA is formed. Your face is turned to the right, both your fists move from behind your back forward and upward, the forearms form a crossed position before your breast. Your left arm is outside, the right arm is inside, the mouth is closed. While breathing out through the nose, you utter a sound "M-M".

Comments: From the position "Two Tigers Cover Up Their Traces" (**Fig.21**), make a step with your left leg to the left and a little forward, at the same time pivot on the right foot to the right by 90 degrees. In such a way you take a stance JI NG MA[36]. Your step is resolute and powerful, the stance is stable and firm, the center of gravity of your body is low. Try to "grasp" the ground with your toes (however, don't bend them). Feel as if no force can move you. After your left foot has been put on the ground, your arms at once move from your back forward and cross before the breast in the position SIN MIN – "An open fan". The arms movement is made rather quickly and with a growing effort, at the same time you breathe out through the nose with a sound "**M-M**". In the final position, the upper part of your spine is slightly bent, the shoulders are moved forward; on the contrary, the thorax is bent inward and lowered a little, the stomach is strained and "filled". At the moment of the biggest effort your breathing is stopped: you "lock" air and set excess pressure in the region of DAANTIN (DANTIAN). However, breathing stops only for a few fractions of a second.

---

[36] *JI NG MA* - it is known in the modern *WUSHU* as the stance "Bow & Arrow".

After it, relax your muscles and breathe out through your nose in a natural way.

Fig.22

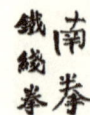

Lam Sai Wing. IRON THREAD.
Southern Shaolin Hung Gar Kung Fu Classics Series

HOI GUNG SE DIU
23. Draw the Bow and Shoot the Eagle

Your feet are in the position JI NG MA. Utter a long sound "EI" through your mouth. Both fists accompanied by the sound move: the left fist (wrist) bends upwards and moves to the left as if you draw a bow, the right fist (wrist) bends downward and draws to the position above the shoulder. You turn your eyes on the left fist.

Comments: In the position SIN MIN JI NG MA (**Fig.22**), raise up your elbows at the level of your shoulders and draw them aside a little. At that time your fists are drawn to the breast, the wrists touch each other as before. At the same time make a long inhalation through your nose. Then, the arms from the position before your breast start moving to both sides in horizontal plane with some strain. At the beginning of the movement the effort is "explosive" in character as if you tear a thick iron wire before your breast and the ends of this wire are wound up around your fists (however, note that your arms move slowly and smoothly, without jerks). This "tearing" effort is accompanied by an expiration through the mouth with a sound "E-I". Then, the arm movement continues with a constant strain and is accompanied by a soundless expiration through your nose. Your fists are tightly clenched, your wrists are bent like a hook in the direction to the inner side of the forearm, you look at your left fist.

卅 三 式

開 弓 射 鵰

鐵 綫 拳

四 六

Fig.23

NGOI BONG SAU
24. An Outward Arms Movement

Your feet are in position JI NG MA. The mouth is closed, you breathe out through the nose and utter a sound "M-M", "M-M", "M-M". The right fist changes its position for JI JEUNG – "A finger and a palm", the left hand is clenched into fist as before. Simultaneously with an expiration through the nose with a sound slowly bend your elbows to bring your hands to your chest. The center of the palm is directed outwards (forward), the fist (wrist) bends inward. You turn your eyes on the left fist.

Comments: Being in the previous position, make a deep inhalation through your nose. At the same time the right fist transforms into the position JI JEUNG - "A finger and a palm" (**Fig.24**). After it the right palm and the left fist with three movements are drawn to the breast and take the position NOI BONG JI - "An inward movement of an arm" (see **Fig. 27**). Each of the three movements is executed with some effort and accompanied by breath out through the nose with a sound "M-M". During pauses between movements muscle strain is decreased, at that moment you can make a very short, shallow inhalation through the nose. Duration of each phase of the movement, including pauses, is about one second or a little longer. After the third inward arms movement, make a complete inhalation through the nose (at that time the thorax slightly rises). Then you immediately proceed to the next technique NGOI BONG SAU YI – "The second outward arms movement" (**Fig.25**).

Fig.24

NGOI BONG SAU YI
25. The Second Outward Arms Movement

Your feet are in the position JI NG MA. The left fist moves and reaches the position before your breast, turns (with its center) downward. Then the right palm in the position JI JEUNG ("A finger and a palm") is moved to the right with a "cutting" movement GOT, at the same time the left fist is moved to the left with a "dividing" movement FAN; you utter a sound "M-M" with your mouth shut. Your face turns to the left, you turn your eyes on the left fist.

Comments: The initial position for this movement is shown in the picture illustrating **Position 27**. Then, with a "tearing" effort your arms start drawing to the left and to the right, at the same time you utter a sound "**M-M**" with your mouth shut. That phase of the movement is shown in the picture illustrating previous position (**Fig.24**). Then, the arms continue drawing to sides slowly and with unchanging strain and take final position (**Fig.25**), at that time you continue breathing out through the nose (soundless).

廿 五 式

外 膀 手 二

鐵 線 拳

五
〇

Fig.25

YAU KIU NOI BONG
26. Soft Bridge From the Inner Side

Your feet are in the position JI NG MA. Close your mouth and utter "M-M", "M-M", "M-M". The right palm in the position JI JEUNG ("A finger and a palm") is drawn back to your chest, at the same time the left fist also comes back to your chest. After it they are slowly pushed forward, the mouth is closed; you breathe out with uttering "M-M".

Comments: From the previous position the arms come back to the breast with three movements and take position before your chest (see **Fig.27**). Each movement is accompanied by a strained expiration through your nose with a sound "**M-M**" (a detailed description see in the comments to **position. 24**). Then, shift your left leg a little to the right and turn about. In such a way you find yourself in the left stance JI NG MY (**Fig.26**). Simultaneously with it, make a full breath in. Then, your elbows descend to ribs, your wrists are crossed, the right palm and the left fist execute a slow and powerful push with a growing effort from the breast forward. The movement is accompanied by an expiration through your nose (mouth is closed). In the final phase (**Fig.26**), when the effort reaches its maximum, an expiration is accompanied by a sound "**M-M**".

Fig.26

NOI BONG JI YI
27. An Inward Movement of an Arm for the Second Time

Your feet are in the position JI NG MA. The right palm in position JI JEUNG – "A finger and a palm" and the left fist come back inside, the movement is accompanied by a sound "A-I".

Comments: You turn about again and take the right stance JI NG MA. During that turn you push with your left elbow to the left and breathe out through the mouth with a sound "A-I" (**Fig.27**).

廿 七 式

內 膀 之 二

鐵 綫 拳

五
四

Fig.27

DING KIU
28. Settled Bridge

Your feet are in the position JI NG MA. The right palm in the position JI JEUNG ("A finger and a palm") moves from the right with a "pressing" movement downward, the left fist raises up into a "supporting" position. You utter a sound "D-I". While continuing (the movement), open your mouth and utter a sound "H-O". The right arm with the palm in the position JI JEUNG straightens downward very slowly and then rises upward.

Comments: You turn about again and come back to the left stance JI NG MA, at the same time you breathe in. At the moment of taking the stance the elbows of both arms descend to ribs, at the same time the left fist starts moving from your breast forward slowly and with some effort and the right palm starts a slow motion from up downward along the side of your body. The stance is firm, your muscles are extremely strained, the left fist "pushes" forward, the right palm "pushes" downward. In the initial phase of the movement you make a short strained expiration with a sound "**D-I**" through the clenched teeth, "lock" air (hold breath), strain abdomen muscles and set heightened pressure in the region of DANTIAN. In the final phase (**Fig.28**) you open your mouth and breathe out with a sound "**H-O**". After it raise your straight right arm on the shoulder level in front of your chest.

式 八 世
訂
橋

鐵
線
拳

五
六

Fig.28

YAU KIU
29. Soft Bridge

From the position JI NG MA the torso turns so that your face is directed straight forward, you proceed to the position YI JI KIM YEUNG MA ("Straddle the Beam with Pincers-Shaped Legs in the Stance of Hieroglyph YI"). The mouth is closed, you utter a sound "M-M". Simultaneously the right JI JEUNG ("A finger and a palm") and the left fist execute a pushing movement forward very slowly.

Comments: Turn to the right by 45 degrees. During the turn the left fist and the right palm are drawn to ribs under your armpits, the elbows are bent and moved back, the shoulders are also moved back, the thorax widens. At the same time, breathe in deeply with your chest and your stomach. Then, without a pause, your arms are straightened (in elbows) slowly and with some strain as if you move away a very heavy thing, at the same time you breathe out through your nose with a sound "**M-M**" (**Fig.29**). Pay special attention to the fact that the general requirements to the stance contained in the comment on **position 9** are valid here and further.

世 九 式

柔

橋

鐵 線 拳

五

八

Fig.29

JE TAU
30. Shield the Head

Your legs are in the position YI JI KIM YEUNG MA. The upper torso turns to the right, the left foot is displaced backward, the toe of the right foot is slightly turned to the right, due to it the stance JI NG MA is formed. You utter a sound "H-E-I" At the same time the right hand changes position for CHYUN JEUNG ("The whole palm"), the center of the palm is turned downward. The right palm, following the transition into the position, moves upward as if it covers the head from above. The left fist delivers a blow "PAAU" (throw away) to the left, you turn your eyes to the left.

Comments: From the previous position, you turn your body to the right by 45 degrees and take right stance JI NG MA. At the same time both arms descend and then move upward, the right palm in the position CHYUN JEUNG ("The whole palm") make a semi-circle in the vertical plane and stops above the head crown, the left fist is moved to the front and upward. The arms movement is slow and strained, in the initial phase expiration is soundless through the nose; in the final phase your mouth is opened a little and you utter "**H-E-E...**". A yell "**...E-I!**" coincides with the maximum effort in the end point of trajectory of arms movement, at that time the thorax slightly descends, all the muscles are extremely strained, the position is stable and firm (**Fig.30**).

式 十 三

頭　　　　遮

戴 䋆 華

六

○

Fig.30

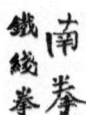

TOK JEUNG
31. Propping Up Palm

Your feet are in the position JI NG MA. The right foot turns inside with its toe, the left toe turns outside; the upper part of your torso from the right-sided position turns straight forward, the upright position SEI PING BAAT FAN MA is formed. The left fist is drawn to the waist, the right palm turns with its center upward and are drawn to the position below the ear and above your shoulder. You utter "T-I" with open mouth.

Comments: From the position JI NG MA you turn your torso to the left by 45 degrees and come to the stance SEI PING BAAT FAN MA [37]. With that the left fist is drawn to the waist, the right palm turns upward and descends to the level of the thigh joint moving along a descending arc with a quick movement, from there it continue moving along ascending arc and stops above the shoulder as shown in the picture (**Fig.31**). The movement is powerful and fast; the work of legs, body and arm is coordinated as if you make a push with a palm from down upward using the force of arm, legs and waist. You make an expiration through the mouth with a sound "**T-I**" in the final phase of the movement.

---

[37] **SEI PING BAAT FAN MA**, literally, "four level and eight parts horse stance", i.e. a low firm stance, the feet are widespread, the center of gravity is situated low.

三 十 一 式

托 掌

鐵 線 拳

六 二

Fig.31

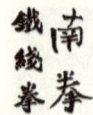

DING GAM KIU
32. A Stable Gold Bridge

Your legs are in the position SEI PING BAAT FAN MA.
The left fist is on your waist as before, in the previous
position, and does not move. From the position above the
shoulder and below the ear, the right palm moves forward
with a pushing movement very slowly. Your mouth utters
"H-O", "H-O", "H-O".

Comments: This position is exactly the same as **position 16**
except that one arm is used here. All requirements to the
movement and to the stance coincide. In this case expiration is
divided into three phases, each phase is accompanied by a
sound "**H-O**" (**Fig.32**).

式 二 十 三

橋 金 定

鐵 線 拳

四 六

Fig.32

Lam Sai Wing. IRON THREAD.
Southern Shaolin Hung Gar Kung Fu Classics Series

鐵 南
綫 拳
拳

JAK SAN CHYUN KIU
33. Incline the Torso and Execute Piercing Bridge

From the position SEI PING BAAT FAN MA, the left toe slightly turns to the left, the right foot with its toe slightly turns inward, the upper part of your body turns to the left, the center of gravity is also shifted to the left; the distinct position JI NG MA is formed. The left fist maintains its position at the waist as before and does not move, the right palm delivers a rapid straight blow to the right. Shout a sound "H-E" with the open mouth.

Comments: A shout "H-E" coincides with the concentration of a piercing effort in the final stage of this movement. Requirements to this kind of a blow are contained in the comment on **position 18,** but the type of expiration somewhat differ: as if you "spit out" some part of air, your teeth are almost clenched, your lips are slightly stretched (**Fig.33**).

式 三 十 三

橋 寸 身 側

鐵 綫 拳

六 六

Fig.33

林
世
崇

鐵南
綫拳
拳

JAI KIU
34. Overpowering Bridge

From the stance JI NG MA, the left foot turns inward, the right foot with its toe turns to the right, the upper part of the body returns to the upright position; the steady position SEI PING BAAT FAN MA is formed. The left fist remains near the waist as before and does not move; the right palm raises up to the level of the ear on one side as if you smooth out your moustache. Then the right palm clenches into fist and lowers with a "bending" movement very slowly, reaches the position before the stomach and stops. Your mouth utters "J-A".

Comments: This movement is described in details in the comment on **position 19**. The difference is that only one (right) arm is used here and the sound **"J-A-A"** accompanying expiration is uttered at the moment of "grasping" movement of the right hand before your breast. Besides, the expiration itself is not so strained as before (the sound is almost the same as that one of "a sigh of relief") (**Fig.34**).

三十四式

制橋

鐵綫拳

六八

Fig.34

Lam Sai Wing. IRON THREAD.
Southern Shaolin Hung Gar Kung Fu Classics Series

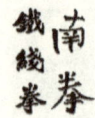

FAN GAM KYUN
35. A Fist Dividing Gold

You stand in the stable position SEI PING BAAT FAN MA. Both fists raise up and cross in a position before the chest, then the fists move to the left and right sides, obliquely downward and outside with "splitting" blows. At the same time you utter "M-M" with the closed mouth. While continuing (expiration), open your mouth, "spit out air" and utter "H-O", "H-O", "H-O" three times. Both fists are drawn back with three movements, simultaneously with the sound.

Stances from the position 22 to the position 35 inclusive are subdivided into left-sided and right-sided. The position SIN MIN ("The fan in front of the face") as well as all "bridges", arms, stances and positions are left-sided, they are similar to the above-described. Unfortunately, we had no possibility to give descriptions and pictures again. We hope that the reader will be able to make sense of it on his own.

Comments: This position (**Fig.35**) fully coincides with **position 20**. Than, you draw fists back to your waist with three movements and take the position YI FU CHIM JUNG – "Two Tigers cover up their traces" (**Fig.21**). All actions are described in detail in the comments on **pos.2** and **pos.21**. After it all movements from **pos.22** to **pos.35** inclusive are executed to the left side: you pivot to the left and take the left stance JI NG MA, your arms are in the position SIN MIN – "The fan in front of your face", the right arm is in front and so on. Thus, the pictures for this series are specular (mirror) reflection of the corresponding pictures from the previous series (**positions 22-35**), they are not available in the original manuscript.

三十五式

分金手

鐵線拳

七〇

Fig.35

Lam Sai Wing. IRON THREAD.
Southern Shaolin Hung Gar Kung Fu Classics Series

SIN MIN SAP JI SAU

36. The Fan of Crossed Arms in Front of the Face

From the stable position SEI PING BAAT FAN MA, your right leg makes a quick step to the right, the left leg follows it, the torso turns to the right and the firm stance JI NG MA is formed. Your mouth is closed, you utter "M-M". Both arms raise up to the position before your face and form a "crossed" position GAAU GA.

Comments: After the execution of movements **22-35** to the right and then to the left side you are in the stance SEI PING BAAT FAN MA (**Fig.35**). Make a step with your left leg to the left and a little forward, at the same time pivot on the right foot to the right by 90 degrees. In such a way you take a right stance JI NG MA. Then your arms move forward and upward and take a "crossed" position before your chest (**Fig.36**), at that time you breathe out through your nose and utter "**M-M**". This position is completely the same as **pos.22** except arms position which is somewhat other (see **Fig.36**). Motion in the stance JI NG MA is quick and stable, your step is resolute and powerful, you may not make "body jumps" (i.e. motion of the torso in the vertical plane), the center of gravity of the body is at the same level all the time.

三 十 六 式

盾 面 十 字 手

鐵 綫 拳

七 二

Fig.36

Lam Sai Wing. IRON THREAD.
Southern Shaolin Hung Gar Kung Fu Classics Series

SEUNG JE SAU
37. A Pair of Covering Hands

You stand in the stable position JI NG MA. Draw down both your fists, unclench them and form the position "palm". Then your palms continue the movement: they move to the left and to the right and raise up along a circle above your head crown. The centers of your palms face down, the left palm is above, the right palm is below. When you execute a covering movement with your hands, you utter "M-M".

Comments: From the previous position SIN MIN SAP JI SAU (**Fig.36**), unclench your fists, the hands in the position "Palm" descend to the thighs, then draw aside and raise up to the position above the head. The hands move in a circle as if you try to embrace a big ball. At the same time, you breathe in through your nose deeply. In the final phase of the movement your arms toughen, the effort is directed downward as if you "press" toward the crown of your head. At the same time you make a short and strained expiration through your nose with a sound "**M-M**", your thorax slightly descends, the abdomen muscles extremely toughen up, your abdomen is "filled" and slightly sticks out (**Fig.37**).

三 十 七 式

雙 遮 手

鐵 線 拳

七 四

Fig.37

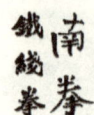

BAAK FU HIN JEUNG
38. The White Tiger Shows its Paws

In the same stance JI NG MA: from the head crown, both palms descend over sides down, move from the right and from the left to the chest and raise up with a "propping up" (TOK) movement. You utter "E-I" through the mouth.

Comments: From the previous position SEUNG JE SAU - "A Pair of Covering Hands" (**Fig.37**), lower your hands to the thighs, transform your palms into the "tiger's claws" and raise your hands up to the position before your chest. This movement is quick and strong as if you push something up, you breathe out sharply, the shout "**E-I**" is loud (**Fig.38**).

三十八式

白虎獻掌

鐵線拳

七六

Fig.38

Lam Sai Wing. IRON THREAD.
Southern Shaolin Hung Gar Kung Fu Classics Series

MAANG FU PA SA
39. The Fierce Tiger Scratches Sand

In the same stance JI NG MA: both palms take the shape of FU JAAU("Tiger's claws") and they are drawn to the left and to the right with a scratching downward movement very slowly. You utter "W-A-A".

Comments: Your hands move downward with a "scratching" effort; muscles of arms, shoulders, back and stomach is toughened. A breath-out through the mouth is long and accompanied with a loud shout "**W-A-A**" (**Fig.39**).

三十九式

猛虎爬沙

鐵綫拳

七八

Fig.39

- 121 -

DING GAM KIU
40. A Stable Gold Bridge

From the position JI NG MA, both feet turn with their toes directed straight forward, your torso pivots into a frontal position, the stance SEI PING BAAT FAN MA[38] is formed. Both palms raise up to the position above your shoulders, they are at the level a little lower than the ears; then they push forward very slowly. You open your mouth and "spit out" air with a sound "HO-O".

Comments: This movement is described in detail above in the comments on **position 16 (Fig.40)**.

---

[38] Here is some discrepancy between the text and the picture: the text says about the stance *SEI PING BAAT FAN MA*, but the picture (Fig.40) shows the stance *YI JI KIM YEUNG MA*. We remind you: feet in the stance *SEI PING BAAT FAN MA* stand apart wider and bent in knees to a higher degree; thus, the center of gravity is low, the stance is very firm and steady.

四 十 武

定 金 橋

峨 螆 拳

八 〇

Fig.40

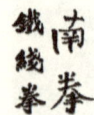

Lam Sai Wing. IRON THREAD.
Southern Shaolin Hung Gar Kung Fu Classics Series

林世榮   鐵線拳 南拳

FU HAAU LUNG YAM
41. Roar of the Tiger and Twitter of the Dragon

In the firm stance SEI PING BAAT FAN MA, the torso descends a little, your legs look like piles driven into the ground, the low position SEI PING BAAT FAN MA is formed. Both palms are drawn to you and turned back to the position above your shoulders and below the level of the your ears. Shake with your palms many times in succession. Utter "E-E-E" with the mouth opened and the teeth clenched.

Comments: This movement is described in detail above in the comments on **position 17** (**Fig.41**).

式 一 十 四

吟 龍 嘯 虎

懾 鎚 牟

八 二

Fig.41

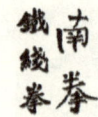

SEUNG CHYUN KIU
42. A Pair of Piercing Bridges

In the low stance SEI PING BAAT FAN MA your torso is slightly raised up, but you maintain the firm position SEI PING BAAT FAN MA. Both palms rush forward with a clap and execute a "piercing" blow BIU, you utter "H-E" through the mouth.

Comments: This movement is described in detail above in the comments on **position 18 (Fig.42)**.

四 十 二 式

雙 寸 橋

鐵 線 拳

八 四

Fig.42

Lam Sai Wing. IRON THREAD.
Southern Shaolin Hung Gar Kung Fu Classics Series

JAI KIU

43. Overpowering Bridges

The stance is SEI PING BAAT FAN MA. Both palms are drawn back and placed low the ears. You separate three joints and clench palms into fists. Then both fists move forward very slowly, at the same time they press downward obliquely. Your mouth is closed, you breathe out and utter a sound "J-A-A".

Comments: This movement is described in details in the comment on **position 19**. The difference is that the sound "**J-A-A**" accompanying expiration is uttered at the moment of "grasping" movement of the hands before your breast. Besides, the expiration itself is not so strained as before (the sound is almost the same as that one of "a sigh of relief") (**Fig.43**).

式 三 十 四

割 橋

鐵 綫 拳

八 六

Fig.43

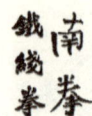

FAN GAM KYUN
44. A Fist Dividing Gold

The position is SEI PING BAAT FAN MA. Both fists from the previous position (Fig.43) are drawn to your breast, your right arm is outside, the left arm is inside. A "crossed" position is formed. The mouth is closed, you utter "M-M" through your nose; simultaneously both fists are drawn to sides with a powerful "splitting" movement. Your eyes are turned forward.

Comments: This movement is described in detail in the comments on **position 20 (Fig.44)**.

四十四式

合全拳

鐵綫拳

八八

Fig.44

Lam Sai Wing. IRON THREAD.
Southern Shaolin Hung Gar Kung Fu Classics Series

YI FU CHIM JUNG

45. Two Tigers Cover Up Their Traces

The position is SEI PING BAAT FAN MA. Both fists from the previous position (Fig.44) draw toward you and backward in three movements, at that time you open your mouth and "spit out" air. Utter "H-O", "H-O", "H-O".

Comments: This movement is described in detail in the comments on **position 2**. See also comments on **position 9** and **position 21** (**Fig.45**).

四十五式

二庚潛踪

鐵線拳

九
〇

Fig.45

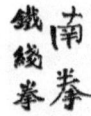

KEI LEUN BOU
46. Unicorn's Step

From the position SEI PING BAAT FAN MA, your left foot advances and stands in front of the right one, the position SIN MIN SEI PING BAAT FAN MA – "A Fan Before the Face in Stable Eight Fen Stance of a Horse" is formed. Both fists raise up from behind and move forward, reach the level of your mouth where they are aligned and stop. A "crossed" position is formed: the right arm is outside, right fist (wrist) is hooked inside; the left arm is inside and press forward to the right arm. You utter "M-M" through the nose.

Execute left and right positions of "A fan before the face", "bridges", arms, steps in the same way, but to the opposite side.

Comments: You are in the stance SEI PING BAAT FAN MA (**Fig.45**). Shift body weight to the right leg; at the same time the left foot moves along an arc from the left to the right, passes in front of the right foot and descends to the ground on the right from the right foot at a distance of one step approximately, its toe is turned to the front. At this moment the heel of the right foot takes off the ground, the main weight of your body is on the left leg. Your knees are brought together, the right knee sets against the calf muscle of the left leg. This method of movement is called KEI LEUN BOU – "Unicorn's step". When moving the left foot, its sole slides over the ground, that means that the foot should not be raised too high. The step is quick, but firm; the legs are bent in knees: in each phase of the movement the center of gravity is at the same height. Then, without stopping in the position KEI LEUN BOU, you turn

about on your soles and take the stance SEI PING BAAT FAN MA. At the same time your arms with an increasing effort move

式六十四

步麟麒

鐵線拳

九二

Fig.46

from your back forward and upward to the position "A fan before the face" (**Fig.46**). In the final phase of the movement you utter "**M-M**" and "lock" air in DAANTIN (DANTIAN) (see details in the comment on **position 22**). Then you repeat **positions** from **36** to **46** inclusive to another side: the right foot steps to the right, the torso turns to the left etc.

GAAP MUK CHEUI
47. To Squeeze Between Wooden Mallets.

From the position SEI PING BAAT FAN MA both feet with their toes turn a little to the left, the upper part of the torso also turn to the left, the position JI NG MA is formed. Both arms move to the left as a single whole, then move forward. The right fist with its center points upward, presses downward according to the position; the left fist with its center points downward, the left arm is bent in elbow and left fist is above the right fist. Utter "M-M".

Comments: Proceed from the previous position (**Fig.46**) to the left stance JI NG MA. At that time breathe in deeply through the nose and at the same time draw fists to your left shoulder with some effort. Then, turn the left fist with its center downward and the right fist with its center upward and slowly move your arms with an increasing effort forward to the position shown in the picture (**Fig.47**). Note that the fists must be tightly clenched and wrists bent; you should feel a "twisting" effort in the sinew of your forearms. In the final phase forward pressing force reaches its maximum and accompanied with a strained expiration with a sound "**M-M**".

四 十 七 式

夫 木 槌

鐵 綫 拳

九 四

Fig.47

TAI WU GING JAU
48. Raise a Jug and Bring Wine

Both feet with their toes turn from position JI NG MA to the right at the same time, the whole torso also turns to the right, the right position JI NG MA is formed. You bend your right arm and draw to yourself, your right fist rises to the level of your ear. The left arm is bent, the left fist turns and follows the movement of (the right) arm. Open your mouth, "spit out" air with a sound "H-O".

Comments: Turn about (by 180 degrees) and take the right stance JI NG MA. At the same time your arms move to the position shown in the picture (**Fig.48**). The fists are tightly clenched as before, wrists bent, arms toughened. Breathe out through your mouth and utter "**H-O**".

四十八式

提壺敬酒

鐵線拳

九六

Fig.48

Lam Sai Wing. IRON THREAD.
Southern Shaolin Hung Gar Kung Fu Classics Series

WAANG GOT SAU
49. A Hand Cutting Across

The stance is JI NG MA as before. Your right fist is risen to the ear and (wrist) bent. Then your (right) fist, while moving downward, unclenches into the position JI JEUNG – "Finger and palm" and draws backward with an oblique cutting movement. Simultaneously, your left arm with "hooked" fist moves to the left and a little upward in a "supporting" position. Your eyes look at the left fist. Utter one sound "M-M" with the closed mouth.

Comments: The initial phase of this movement is shown in **Fig.27**, the final phase in **Fig.49** (see also the comment on **position 25**).

Fig.49

NOI BONG SAU
50. An Inward Movement of an Arm

The stance is JI NG MA. The left arm with the bent fist (wrist) in a "supporting" position and the right "Finger and palm" move inward with a very slow "clasping" movement. You close your mouth and utter "M-M", "M-M", "M-M". Arms movement accompanies the sound.

Comments: This movement is described in detail in comment on **position 24**. In this case the only difference is in the initial position of the right arm: it is almost completely straightened in elbow (see **Fig.49**) and correspondingly the trajectory of its movement is somewhat longer **(Fig.50)**.

五 十 式

內 膀 手

鐵 綫 拳

一〇〇

Fig.50

Lam Sai Wing. IRON THREAD.
Southern Shaolin Hung Gar Kung Fu Classics Series

NOI BONG YAU KIU
51. To Move Inward the Soft Bridge

*At first you turn from the position JI NG MA and take
the position SEI PING BAAT FAN MA. During a left turn
the left fist and the right "finger and palm" also move to
the left and then take the position under armpits. From
armpits both hands push forward very slowly. Utter "M-
M" with the closed mouth.*

Comments: Turn from the right position JI NG MA to the left
by 90 degrees and take the stance SEI PING BAAT FAN MA.
This movement is explained in detail in the comment on
position 29 (Fig.51).

式 一 十 三

内 膝 柔 橋

鐵 線 拳

一 〇 二

Fig.51

Lam Sai Wing. IRON THREAD.
Southern Shaolin Hung Gar Kung Fu Classics Series

NOI BONG YAU KIU
52. To Move Inward the Soft Bridge

At first turn from the an balanced position SEI PING BAAT FAN MA to the left position JI NG MA. During a turn to the stance the left fist and the right "finger and palm" are also drawn to armpits, then push forward very slowly. Close your mouth and utter "M-M".

Comments: Turn by 90 degrees to the left and take left stance JI NG MA, at the same time you make a full inhalation and draw the left fist and the right palm to armpits (at that time the palm turns, with its forefinger downward). Then the right palm and the left fist execute a slow and powerful push from your breast forward with an increasing effort. The movement is accompanied by an expiration through your nose. In the final phase **(Fig.52)**, when the effort reaches its maximum the expiration is accompanied by a sound "**M-M**".

第 三 十 二 式

內 膀 柔 橋

鐵 線 拳

一〇四

Fig.52

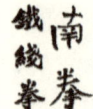

Lam Sai Wing. IRON THREAD.
Southern Shaolin Hung Gar Kung Fu Classics Series

JE TAU
53. Shield the Head

At first you turn from the left stance JI NG MA to the right stance JI NG MA. The left fist moves to the left side and (the arm) straightens. The right palm with joined fingers rises above your head crown into a "protective" position, the palm center points downward. You utter "HE-A".

Comments: This movement is explained in detail in the comment on **position 30**. There is some difference in character of expiration (and, accordingly, the sound): you utter **"HE-A"** **(Fig.53)**.

式 三 十 五

遞 頭

鐵線拳

一〇六

Fig.53

Lam Sai Wing. IRON THREAD.
Southern Shaolin Hung Gar Kung Fu Classics Series

TOK SAU
54. Propping Up Hand

At first turn from the right stance JI NG MA to the balanced stance SEI PING BAAT FAN MA. The left fist is drawn to your waist, the right palm in a circle lowers and then rise with a "supporting" movement again. You utter "H-E" with your mouth.

Comments: This movement is explained in detail in the comment on **position 31**. There is some difference in character of expiration (and, accordingly, the sound): here it is shorter and sharper – "**H-E**" **(Fig.54)**.

五十四式

托手

鐵綫拳

一〇八

Fig.54

 Lam Sai Wing. IRON THREAD.
Southern Shaolin Hung Gar Kung Fu Classics Series

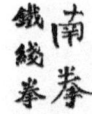

FU HAAU LUNG YAM
55. Roar of the Tiger and Twitter of the Dragon

As before, you are in the balanced position SEI PING BAAT FAN MA. The left fist moves directly forward and rises to the level of your face, the left arm straightens, (then) the right palm rises at once and takes position above your shoulder. Open your mouth, clench teeth and utter "E-E-E".

Comments: Sink a little down in the stance SEI PING BAAT FAN MA. Immediately after it the left fist starts moving from down upward and forward, the movement is slow and strained, expiration is soundless through the nose (imagine that you raise up a pail with water). Stop your fist at the level of the chin, quickly breathe in through your nose. Immediately the right fist unclenches and the palm is moved to the position above your shoulder with fast movement. Then, shake your right hand above your shoulder several times, as if a "gust of the wind swings a willow". In that time make a long strenuous breath out through your mouth. At that moment your teeth are almost clenched, your lips are stretched, the position of the tongue and the vocal chords corresponds to the position when one pronounces the sound "**E-E**" (as in "bed"), but due to a strong thrust of expired air the sound is like rather something between whistle and hiss **(Fig.55)**.

武 五 十 五

吟 龍 嘯 虎

鐵 綫 拳

一一〇

Fig.55

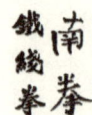

CHYUN KIU
56. Piercing Bridge

In the stance SEI PING BAAT FAN MA the left toe slightly turns to the left, the right toe slightly turns inward, the upper part of your torso turns to the left, the center of gravity shifts to the left side; at once you turn from the stance SEI PING BAAT FAN MA to the left stance JI NG MA. The left fist is drawn to the waist, the right palm with joined fingers executes a "piercing" blow BIU strictly to the right. The movement is accompanied by a sound "HIT".

Comments: This position is fully identical to **position 33**. The only difference is in the sound uttered during a blow delivered with finger tips. See details in the comments on **position 6**, **position 18** and **position 33 (Fig.56)**.

五十六式

橋 寸

鐵綫拳

一
一
二

Fig.56

Lam Sai Wing. IRON THREAD.
Southern Shaolin Hung Gar Kung Fu Classics Series

鐵 南
綫 拳
拳

JAI KIU

57. Overpowering Bridge

In the left stance JI NG MA turn the toe of the left foot a little inward, the toe of the right foot outward, the upper part of the torso turns strictly forward and returns to the upright position SEI PING BAAT FAN MA. The left fist is near your waist as before and does not move, the right arm "bends three joints", clenches into fist at the level of your shoulder, then very slowly lowers with a "pressing" movement. Utter a sound "E-I" with your mouth.

Comments: This movement is explained in detail in the comment on **position 34 (Fig.57)**.

制 橋 五 十 七 式

鐵 線 拳

一 一 四

Fig.57

FAN GAM CHEUI
58. A Blow Dividing Gold

Both fists in the firm stance SEI PING BAAT FAN MA rise to a position before your chest and form a "crossed" position. The right fist is hooked inside, the left fist with its center also points inward and presses forward (on the right fist). Then, both fists draw to both sides simultaneously with a "overhanging" blow GWA[39]. Utter "M-M".

Execute left and right positions of "A fan before the face", "bridges", arms, steps in the same way, but to the opposite side.

Comments: This movement is explained in detail in the comment on **position 35 (Fig.58)**.

Then you repeat **positions** from **46** to **58** inclusive to another side: the right foot steps to the left ("Unicorn's Step"), the torso turns to the left etc.

---

[39] *GUA KYUN*, or "Overhanging Fist", is a blow (or a block) with the back side of a fist and (or) the outer side of forearm delivered from up to down; the fist moves from the shoulder to the waist making a semi-circle in the vertical plane.

五 十 八 式

分 金 搥

鐵 綫 拳

一 一 六

Fig.58

 Lam Sai Wing. IRON THREAD.
Southern Shaolin Hung Gar Kung Fu Classics Series

SAP JI SAU
59. Cross Hands

Your right leg makes one step forward from the (stance)
SEI PING BAAT FAN MA ("Four Level and Eight Parts
Horse Stance), the left leg follows (the right one), at that
time you proceed (to the stance) YI JI KIM YEUNG MA
("Straddle the Beam with Pincers-Shaped Legs in the
Stance of Hieroglyph YI"). Both fists move forward and
upward from behind your back along both sides from the
left and the right and form a "crossed" position. The
centers of both fists are turned inside, the right fist is
hooked and outside, the left fist presses the right one from
inside. Utter "M-M".

Comments: You are in the stance SEI PING BAAT FAN MA.
Your right leg steps forward, then the left leg follows the right
one. In such a way you advance by one step and proceed to the
position YI JI KIM YEUNG MA. (**We remind you: feet in the
stance SEI PING BAAT FAN MA stand apart wider and legs
bent in knees to a higher degree; thus, the center of gravity is
low, the stance is very firm and steady.**) Your step is resolute
and powerful, your soles glide over the ground, the knees do
not straighten. You stare ahead. When your left foot touches the
ground, your arms move forward and upward with some effort
to the position SAP JI SAU (**Fig.59**). At the same time you
make a short and strained expiration through your nose with a
sound "**M-M**", your thorax slightly descends, the abdomen
muscles extremely toughen up, your abdomen is "filled" and
slightly sticks out. In this case expiration and position is similar
to that one described in the comment on **position 10**.

五十九式

十字手

鐵線拳

二一八

Fig.59

Lam Sai Wing. IRON THREAD.
Southern Shaolin Hung Gar Kung Fu Classics Series

JE TIN
60. Shield the Sky

Your legs are in the position YI JI KIM YEUNG MA. Both fists change their form and become JI JEUNG ("Finger and Palm"), the centers of both palms turn forward. The right palm is outside as before and hooked (in wrist), the left palm presses forward from inside (to the right palm); the "crossed" position is still preserved. Your arms rise and reliably protect your head. Open your mouth, "spit out" muddy air and at the same time utter "H-O".

Comments: This position is fully identical to **position 12**. The only difference is in character and sound of expiration ("**H-O**"): it is shorter and curt in this case **(Fig.60)**.

六 十 式

遮 天

鐵 線 拳

一 三 〇

Fig.60

FEI NGAAN LIN YIK
61. A Flying Goose Flaps Its Wings

Your legs are in the position YI JI KIM YEUNG MA. The palms raised above the head are separated and lowered from left and right to your pelvis with a "cutting" downward movement. Utter "H-E" through your mouth.

Comments: This arms movement is described in detail in the comment on **position 5**. The only difference is in the initial position (compare **Fig.4** and **Fig.60**) **(Fig.61)**.

Fig.61

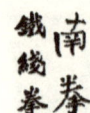

Lam Sai Wing. IRON THREAD.
Southern Shaolin Hung Gar Kung Fu Classics Series

MEI WU HIN JEUNG
62. Mei Wu Hands a Staff

From the left and right, both palms move in front of the torso upward with a "supporting" movement and reach a position at the shoulder level. Utter "E-I" during hands movement.

Comments: Arms movement is quick and strong as if you push something upward (see comments to **Position 15**). Your yell is curt and loud: "**E-I**" (**Fig.62**).

Fig.62

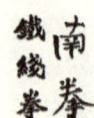

SEUNG JE TAU
63. Shield the Head with Both (Hands)

Your legs are in the position YI JI KIM YEUNG MA. Both palms move to the left and to the right to ribs from the position before the shoulders and lower, then, at once they move upward again. The centers of the palms are turning downward, the palms are above your head against each other in an open position and protect the head. Utter "HE-A" through your mouth.

Comments: The palms lower to the level of the thigh joint, then, without interrupting movement, they move to the right and to the left and upward into a position above your head. The hands move along a circle as if you embrace a big ball. In the final phase of the movement your arms toughen, the effort is directed downward as if you press toward the crown of your head; at that time you make a prolonged expiration through your mouth with a sound "H-E", it ends with a vigorous and short shout "A!". Simultaneously with that the thorax slightly lowers, the muscles of your stomach extremely toughen, the stomach is "filled" and protruded a little **(Fig.63)**.

弍三十六

雙遮頸

鐵線拳

一二六

Fig.63

BAAK KIU
64. Push with Bridges

Your legs are in the position YI JI KIM YEUNG MA. Both palms move to the left and to the right from a position above your head and lower down and back; then, at once they rise from the left and from the right before the breast with a "supporting" movement, the centers of the palms face up; the position BAAK KIU – "Press (push) with bridges" is formed. Utter "HAI" through your mouth.

Comments: From the position above the head (**Fig.63**), your hands with a circular movement lower through sides to the level of thigh joint. Then they, without stopping, rise to a "supporting" position on the level of your shoulders. The movement is quick and strong as if you make a upward push from down (**Fig.64**).

式 四 十 彡

橋　　　逼

鐵　線　拳

一二八

Fig.64

DING GAM KIU
65. A Stable Gold Bridge

Your legs are in the position YI JI KIM YEUNG MA. At first, both palms rise and take position near the ears, then they move forward very slowly and make push with four fingers. When straightening your arms, utter "H-O", "H-O", "H-O".

Comments: This position fully coincides with **position 16**. All requirements and recommendations in the text and in the comment on this position are effective in this case. The only difference is that now during expiration you utter the sound **"H-O"** three times. **(Fig.65)**.

二 十 五 式

足 金 橋

鐵線拳

一三〇

Fig.65

Lam Sai Wing. IRON THREAD.
Southern Shaolin Hung Gar Kung Fu Classics Series

SEUNG CHYUN KIU
66. A Pair of Piercing Bridges

Your legs are in the position YI JI KIM YEUNG MA. Both palms draw back, the elbows lower a little, four fingers of both hands close together and stretch horizontally, in such a way hands form the position "full palm". Then the hands move forward with a "piercing" blow BIU. Utter "E-I!" through the mouth.

Comments: This movement is described in detail in the comment on **position 18** (only in this case the height of the stance does not change) **(Fig.66)**.

与 十 二 式

儯 寸 橋

Fig.66

SAP JI SAU
67. Cross Hands

You are in the position YI JI KIM YEUNG MA, both arms are stretched forward. You bend three joints[40], clench your hands into fists and draw fists to the chest. The centers of both fists face inside. The right fist is outside and hooked inside; the left fist press from inside forward. Both fists form a "crossed" position. At the same time utter "M-M".

Note: First of all, it should be pointed out that in this place the original Chinese edition shows a figure for **position 17** and **position 41** - "Roar of the Tiger and Twitter of the Dragon". It does not conform with the position name and explanation to it. It may be only suggested that figures were mixed up during type-setting and that was the cause of this non-conformance. We took the liberty to show in this place the figure for **position 59** with same name (SAP JI SAU – "Cross Hands") instead of figure for **position 17** or **position 41** in the original.

Comments: After delivering a "piercing" blow BIU the palms clench into fists and they are drawn, with some effort, to the breast to be in a "crossed" position **(Fig.67)**.

---

[40] "To bend three joints" means to bend an arm in shoulder, elbow and wrist joints.

式 七 十 与
十 字 手

鐵 綫 拳

一 三 〇

Fig.67

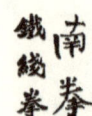

Lam Sai Wing. IRON THREAD.
Southern Shaolin Hung Gar Kung Fu Classics Series

鐵 南
綫 拳
拳

FAN GAM KYUN
68. A Fist Dividing Gold

At first, from the stance YI JI KIM YEUNG MA, you lower yourself into the stance SEI PING BAAT FAN MA. At that time, from a crossed position of the arms before the chest, both fists are simultaneously drawn to both sides with a "splitting" movement. Utter "M-M".

Comments: This movement was described in detail in the comment on **position 20**. The only difference is that in this case, while drawing the fists aside and downward with a "splitting" movement, you proceed to a lower stance and by it reinforce arms action due to body weight **(Fig.68)**.

古十八式

分金拳

鐵線拳

一三六

Fig.68

Lam Sai Wing. IRON THREAD.
Southern Shaolin Hung Gar Kung Fu Classics Series

YI FU CHIM JUNG
69. Two Tigers Cover Up Their Traces

You return from the stance SEI PING BAAT FAN MA
back to the stance YI JI KIM YEUNG MA. Both fists with
three separate movements draw back with some effort.
You open your mouth and "spit out" "muddy" air with
uttering "H-O", "H-O", "H-O".

Comments: The arms movement and technique of breath are
described in the comment on **position 2**. The **Fig.45** shows a
side view **(Fig.69)**.

第六十九式

二虎潛蹤

鐵線拳

一三八

Fig.69

Lam Sai Wing. IRON THREAD.
Southern Shaolin Hung Gar Kung Fu Classics Series

GING LAI SAU SIK
70. A Greeting Gesture and Final Position

Both fists in the position "Two Tigers cover up their traces" draw to behind your back with three separate movements. After it both fists return back along sides and move forward. The left fist opens into the position "palm" and rises together with the right fist to the level opposite the nose tip. The left foot is lightened and "suspended", the right foot stands firmly. This position is similar to the first position GING LAI – "Greeting". This exercise complex starts and ends with it.

***

式 十 七

收 式

鐵 綫 拳

一八〇

Fig.70

Shaolin Kung Fu Online Library
www.kungfulibrary.com

Chinese Martial Arts - Theory & Practice
Old Chinese Books, Treatises, Manuscripts

Lam Sai Wing. Moving Along the Hieroglyph Gung, I Tame the Tiger with the Pugilistic Art.

Lam Sai Wing. Tiger and Crane Double Form.

Lam Sai Wing. TID SIN: Iron Thread.

Jin Jing Zhong. Training Methods of 72 Arts of Shaolin.

Jin Jing Zhong. Dian Xue Shu: Skill of Acting on Acupoints.

Liu Jin Sheng. CHIN NA FA: Skill of Catch and Hold.

Tang Ji Ren. Pugilistic Art of the Tang Family. DA HONG QUAN.

Xu Yi Qian. CHUAN NA QUAN: Style of Piercing Blows and Holds.

Yuan Chu Cai. MEI HUA ZHUANG: Poles of Plum Blossom. External and Internal Training.

 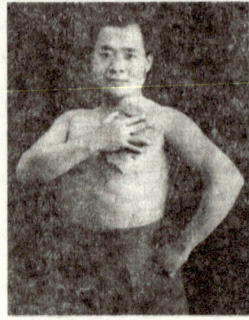 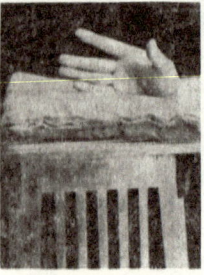

www.ingramcontent.com/pod-product-compliance
Lightning Source LLC
Chambersburg PA
CBHW021150130626
46554CB00005B/1746